CW00816154

GREAT
CARP STORIES

GREAT
CARP STORIES

JON BERRY

2012
THE MEDLAR PRESS
ELLESMERE

Published by The Medlar Press Limited,
The Grange, Ellesmere, Shropshire SY12 9DE
www.medlarpress.com

ISBN 978-1-907110-00-9

First published 2012

Introduction, selection and notes © Jon Berry and Jon Ward-Allen 2012

Design © The Medlar Press 2012

Designed and typeset in $11^{1}/_{2}$ on 14pt Bembo Roman

Produced in England by The Medlar Press Limited,
Ellesmere, England.

Contents

Contents

Introduction

Readers of a certain vintage - those who remember black and white television, sherbet dips and the legitimate use of the shoulder charge in football - will probably recall that almost every boy in England would claim a perch as his first fish. The larger species - tench, pike, and the almost mythical carp - were dreamt of, but belonged to the wise old men in green who lurked on the other side of the pond. We all wanted to catch these fabulous fish, of course, but knew that an apprenticeship had to be first served among the obliging stripeys.

So much has changed; many a new angler, young or otherwise, begins with carp. The rods, reels, rigs and bait are easily obtained, and decades have passed since anyone has solder-blobbed their salmon hooks or constructed prodigious landing-nets from bicycle wheels and potato sacks. Carp angling, once the preserve of secretive, inventive men with the patience to blank, if required, from one end of the season to the other, can now be purchased 'off the shelf'.

There is much to lament in this. Old-timers (and I am slowly beginning to acknowledge that I may be one of them) complain that nobody knows how to shot a stick float or stret-peg a river anymore. We struggle to say the word 'bivvie' without a dismissive tone, rage against the overt consumerism of it all, and develop a mild allergy towards things that bleep, buzz or are unnecessarily camouflaged. Bait boats can have us foaming at the mouth.

And yet, carp fishing thrives like no other branch of the sport. Its most celebrated practitioners are technically-gifted, innovative and dedicated souls. Improvements in fish care have arisen solely from carp anglers' love for their quarry, while advances in terminal tackle and rigs throughout the sport again evolved from the minds of these men. For many, carp fishing may resemble a circus, but if this is so then it is one with many magicians and few clowns. For most, carp fishing is still about misty mornings, a mercurial quarry, uncaught giants and the overwhelming joy found in silent expectation.

The stories here reflect, I hope, the breadth of carp fishing's unique appeal. They offer haunted pools, giant fish, a little bit of history and triumph and tragedy in equal measure. Some of the authors are celebrated heroes of the sport, while others may be unknown, as yet, to the reader. There are contributions from members of the original Carp Catchers' Club and a smattering of Victorian pioneers, but far

less from the modern specimen hunters. Readers with
an interest in the latter are urged to investigate the
publications of *The Carp Society* – for examples of
the best modern carp writing, they have yet to be
bettered.

Carp fishing has a rich literary heritage, and no
anthology could include every great account of lost or
captured monsters. The first Medlar carp anthology,
Shadows and Reflections, included many of the best-
known and well-loved tales, and so this collection has
probed a little deeper into the more obscure corners
of the genre. I resisted the temptation to include an
account of my first thirty-pounder, a fish which succeeded in breaking a friend's prized cane rod and
stripping the gears in my old Mitchell reel, and which
led to a near-cataclysmic row with my then girlfriend.
Perhaps, if a third carp anthology ever bubbles to the
surface, that tale will be told. For now, here are some
great carp stories – I do hope you enjoy them.

Jon Berry, October 2012.

The Carpe

Leonard Mascall

The carpe also is a straunge and daintie fish to take, his baites are not well knowne, for he hath not long beene in this realme. The first bringer of them into England (as I have beene credibly enformed) was maister Mascoll of Plumsted in Sussex, who also brought first the planting of the Pippin in England: but now many places are replenished with carpes, both in poundes and rivers, and because not knowing well his cheefe baites in each moneth, I will write the lesse of him, he is a straunge fish in the water, and very straunge to byte, but at certaine times to wit, at foure a clocke in the morning, and eight at night be his chiefe byting times, and he is so strong enarmed in the mouth, that no weake harnesse will hold him, and his byting is very tickle: but as touching his baytes, having small knowledge by experience, I am loth to write more then I know and have prooved. But well

I wote, the red worme and the meno bee good baites for him in all times of the yeare, and in June with the cadys or water worme: in July and in August with the maggot or gentyll, and with the coale worme, also with paste made with hony and wheate flower, but in Automne, with the redde worme is best, and also the grashopper with his legs cut off, which he wil take in the morning, or the whites of hard egges steeped in tarte ale, or the white snaile.

A Welsh Carp Lake

H. T. Sheringham

It may be true that Wales rises to greater heights elsewhere, as the natives of the valley aver; but the fair-minded man, whose opinions are not warped by the magnificence of the unknown, would admit yon steeps to be mountains, be there never so many Snowdons in the next county but one. The proof of the mountain is in the climbing, after all, and the natives of the valley do not climb. With that instinct begotten of surroundings which passes very well for wisdom, they remain firmly in the valley, for the most part leaning on the bridge and watching two small trout in the river below - the only trout in the river below. This is another point on which the natives and the fair-minded man will disagree; for, while they assert roundly that there are other, several other, trout in the stream, he knows that this is not the case, for the proof of trout is in the catching, and samlets don't count. The other trout, it is fair to assume, are among the Snowdons in the next county but one.

This is the principal reason why the local mountains have to be faced and overcome. Three good leagues to the east lies a fair sheet of water full of large trout and massive carp, which have never been angled for within memory of native man. The March brown is the fly, and a big basket is a certainty - so says local wisdom as it leans on the parapet. These are just the innocent fish that a fond fancy had conjured up in London chambers, though it had not estimated the mountains to be so high or the leagues so long; in the metropolis a mountain comes vaguely before one's mental vision as something after the pattern of Primrose Hill, while a league is merely twenty minutes' drive in the direction of West Kensington. These conceptions, of course, prove to be inadequate, and it takes two good hours quite fully occupied on steep and slippery turf and amid prickly gorse-bushes. However, the tableland of the second mountain is at last attained, the two miles of comparatively level ground are covered with greater ease, and the lake comes into view. It is not large - about a quarter of a mile across - is almost round, and absolutely treeless, except for two or three shrubs that grow on a little island near the farther shore. The prevailing note in the colouring is yellow; the sun shines yellow, the banks are yellow, and the bottom is yellow. In the foreground, however, is a touch of black - a small boathouse, of which the men of the valley said nothing. There is no boat in it, and its use is not clear. There is no house in miles, and it seems a long distance to come for a row, especially if there is no boat to row in when you get there. Perhaps some sportsman once thought of establishing an estate up here, and began with the boathouse; or perhaps it is not a boathouse at all, but something to do with druids, and of greater age than it looks; or perhaps - but this is irrelevant, and the tackle must be put together.

The large trout spoken of are more important than carp, and the outfit is better suited for their capture, for no bottom-fishing tackle was brought into Wales. Accordingly, March brown, coch-y-bondhu, and Greenwell's glory are soon searching the edge of the lake; no rises can be seen, but a nice ripple inspires hope, and the gradual circuit of the shore is begun. Not a trout takes the least notice of the flies, though an occasional wallow a long way out betrays carp, and after much toil and tread it becomes clear that if there are trout here they are not rising - an opinion which gradually mellows to the certainty that there are no trout here to rise. As the point opposite the little island

is approached the water becomes much shallower,
and the signs of carp more numerous, until at last, in
eighteen inches of water, several can plainly be seen
swimming lazily about, some fifteen yards from
the shore. From force of habit the March brown,
coch-y-bondhu, and Greenwell's glory are despatched
in pursuit of them, of course without result. The fish
display neither interest nor alarm, but merely indif-
ference. It is time to adopt other measures. In the creel
is a large lump of paste made of flour and honey, and
in the fly-book are hooks. Float there is none, but in
this shallow water it is not necessary, and might even
be a hindrance. The only difficulty is to get the bait
out far enough; honey-paste is not the best thing to
cast with a ten-foot fly-rod, and many pellets are scattered about experimentally. Finally, it is proven that
fifteen yards is too ambitious a distance, and an effort
is made to swing a large lump out ten.

This is many yards too few now, for the carp have
gone away to mark their disapproval of the violent
proceedings on the bank; but it is successful, and the
honey-paste settles safely on the bottom, a patch of
white against the yellow. Perhaps the fish will come
back again, though, and a dozen pellets of paste are
thrown out to entice them. A seat is taken on the
yellow bank, the rod is propped in a crevice, and

patience is invoked to aid in the waiting. Patience, after a reasonable time, suggests lunch, which is eaten with an eye on the specks of white. After lunch follows a pipe, and still the specks of white remain undisturbed. Now and again the appearance of a back fin or the tip of a tail shows that the carp are satisfied with their new position twenty-five yards out, and not one seems disposed to return. An hour passes in waiting, and from time to time throwing pellets, so that there is a chain of them between the hook-bait and the fish. A reasonable carp should easily find its way to the big piece that gleams pre-eminent in size and attractiveness.

But all is in vain, apparently, and at last patience goes away again. With it wanders attention, and only instinct remains on guard. Instinct it is that recalls the eye to its duty. The line is tightening, and the large lump of paste is invisible. The rod is picked up, and immediately bends prettily to the run of a good fish, and the light check on the winch makes cheering music. But a carp of three pounds does not seriously endanger the tackle, though it fights gamely enough on a light fly-rod, and a not unduly prolonged contest ends satisfactorily with net and spring-balance. The fish is three pounds one ounce, plump enough, but rather pale in complexion, owing, no doubt, to the colour of his abode, and it has taken not much more than two hours to catch him. This is well enough as carp go, but it is not quite what might have been looked for on a virgin water, nor is the subsequent record of two fish of about the same size in the next three hours quite satisfying. However, it is better than looking at the two small trout in the river, and nine pounds of carp are enough to carry across nine miles of mountain. The return is begun betimes, for it is well not to be benighted in a strange country. Not a trout has been seen to rise all day, and this is explained by the fact that the trout, somewhat magniloquently spoken of by wisdom on the bridge, is dead. There lies his head on the bank - the head of a full five-pounder. How he died is a mystery, but it is sad for a virgin water when its only trout is taken away from it. He is a real loss, and the lake is left with somewhat saddened steps. Henceforward there will be but two trout in the neighbourhood, and life is uncertain.

Carp and their Curious Habits

Frans Domhof

King carp in lakes have some of the most astonishing ways of behaving. Ever since the last war I have been stalking and watching as much as fishing for them. I have had the good fortune to be able to do so in both private and non-fished waters, and in heavily fished club waters or public waters. The latter two have offered me the easiest fishing, the former couple the best watching. One thing, and this has struck me particularly, I have found all these waters to have in common: while in their open stretches the carp were as shy and cautious as indeed the fish are said to be; once within their sanctuary of reeds and plants and lily-pads they were not so easily frightened at all. I have in fact taken them under what must have been thought impossible conditions. I will say this: I believe the carp of the little-fished lakes more shy, but less cautious than those of, say, public waters. By this I mean that they panic quicker, yet also quieten down quicker. And that, while of course the fish of both type of waters are very much creatures of habit, the former show less fear of the angler's gear than do the latter. Also, that if the bait is taken, it will be done with far greater confidence. It will be noticed, however, that I say if, for that is just about it. I have seen a carp, and I am talking about large fish only, hovering over a potato bait, moving away a couple of inches and coming back again for nearly two hours! I guessed him at fully 25lb and I was waiting with my tongue in my cheek, standing like a statue up to my hips in between the reeds. After that time I could no longer stand still for fear of becoming unwell, and regretfully yet relieved once I had made the decision I waded out through the reeds and scrambled ashore. It was only after I had been resting, for a couple of minutes at least, before the big fish seemed to think there was something queer going on. It, too, had been in the reeds like myself and no more than 12 feet away from me. And I did not leave the water very quietly for at that moment it did not matter anymore anyway. Only then did he make off and even so only for some 20 yards, keeping to the outside edge of the reeds in the shallow water.

Another time I was using the only boat and had

moored to reeds not very far from the same place. My
tackle I had cast out in a small bay with a sandy bottom and about 3 feet of water. The bait, consisting of
rather hard bread paste, I had thrown out some 20
yards, no more, and it was absolutely windless. Towards evening I saw some movement in the tall reeds
opposite me across the little bay and I kept alert. I had,
hooked and landed carp from this spot before and
knew that as soon as they felt the hook they would,
for some reason or other, directly make for the open
water, which was very nice going by the best of standards.

After an hour or so I had worked myself up to a
dangerous pitch and I was expecting a bite any time
then. This may sound unbelievable, nevertheless it is
quite true and many times my highly expectant feelings have not proved to be groundless. To be truthful
I should state I had perhaps just as many times when
they did not prove to be the forerunner of a bite only
these are usually not remembered. In any case, this
time nothing came of it. It so happened that at the
other end of the lake a couple of young fellows took
off their clothes and went for a swim. I had seen nothing else than the water near me and my tackle and I
only noticed something was amiss when I felt the
very slight swell from the ruckus the boys must have

kicked up at the other end. At precisely that same instant the carp must have felt it too and what is more the fish must have been almost upon my bait, for the moment I saw what was going on I saw a great swirl in the shallow water just where the paste had been placed by me. The carp apparently was alarmed and left at an enormous speed, a heavy wake following him towards the deeper parts.

The very next morning the fish, and several others with him, slowly cruised about across the same bay; they would have none of any paste. Great big fish they were and I was anxious to get one of them. After a while I could not detect them nor their presence any more and out of curiosity more than anything else I cast the boat loose and started to slowly pole through the shallower part of the lake. They were there all right and they moved away in front of the boat, some 20 to 30 yards out. Never mind how careful I went on, they kept sort of out of distance. I thought the better of it and settled down again and I cast the paste-ball far this time, near on 50 yards in front of the boat on the same course I had been poling. I might as well have gone home, for all I got was a terrific headache from the glaring sun on the surface of the water.

This same lake yielded me a nice 20-pounder all the same. Bubbling, one of the things by which one may detect the presence of the fish, is hardly ever seen, though they betray themselves by, even if not often, jumping clear out of the water, always there where the bottom gradually starts to slope from a depth of 2 to 9 feet at the extreme. Always, too, this jumping takes place at the north-easterly side of the lake. One morning, still before sun up I remember, I had just put in my groundbait and settled down for the usual length of time till it became too warm when I saw and heard a large carp jump. It was still and the water lay like a mirror. For some time, possibly only a couple of minutes, I wondered, and then I thought I would have a try. Just then the fish, or one very much like the first one, had another jump and I could see he had moved nearer the reeds, about 10 feet out. Big bubbles were still floating about at the spot when I tied the boat fast to the reeds some 10 yards away. I hoped that even if I did not get a pull from him, perhaps he would take to the air once more and then I might be able to see or detect something or other which would put me in touch with the unknown cause which makes these huge fish jump like trout. I am sure I had not waited longer than five minutes when I saw a wake coming towards my bait and I thought it to be coming from a heavy pike. It was the carp, however; he must have moved off farther than I had anticipated, for a second or two after, the bait was taken and I securely hooked him; after a while the fish was duly netted. This one did not seem too shy.

Since then I have, of course, always had a soft spot for these jumpers, but I have not taken many of them out in the open. I have, though, when close to the bank or in between the reeds. In fact, I often leave home rather early in the afternoon for an evening's carping, only to walk about and see if I can spot any very coloured water in the shallows. These big ones kick up a good bit of sand or mud and it is often rather easy to see where one did and half the time I have found them willing takers. The exception, always encountered, presents itself here too. That is when carp start to jump madly all over the place. They seem to lose all precaution then and often get landed right up on top of the reeds, to be seen clearly in detail for everyone. Twice I have put back carp after they had got themselves altogether stranded and were in fact jumping about madly on the grass bank. I believe this activity due to sexual excitement in some way, but I have only noticed it in water where carp do not spawn. Why this should be I do not know, it may be that because of this failure the fish get up to these antics. Certainly it is heart-breaking for an angler sitting amidst them and having his line shoved about like nobody's business and not getting a bite at all. It is after happenings like these the big stories may be heard!

I remember, too, a club water where any angler may fish the day for the sum of roughly one shilling. I had been fishing from a boat at the very same place for several days and I was determined to get a carp here. Every morning I would pack up my gear about mid-day to return later in the afternoon. One particular morning I again had failed to interest any fish and had poled back the boat towards its mooring place near the house of the keeper. As I made it fast by the rope hanging from the bow, my reel, a Rapidex, screamed; the water is very shallow there, only about 1 foot, and I turned in time to see a great commotion and then the reel was silent. The hook did not take hold of its own accord and the carp was gone. The potato covering the hook must have fallen overboard unnoticed and here in the shallows, touched the ground, or else the carp mistook himself for a pike and thought the trolled spud a spoon. Whatever might be the case, this huge fish took the bait in less water than his own height measurements. No plants or weeds here either.

This same water twice offered me some fish - although they were smaller and the largest one was only 12lb - in a most shocking way. I had gone over to just look about and have a chat with the keeper, who was a great angler in his day and four times champion of the northern province of Friesland, from where the famed Friesian cattle come. We passed the time of day and then we both saw the reeds moving about as if being parted by a large unseen comb. Here too the water was no more than 3 feet in depth and I regretted not bringing any tackle; always should a fisherman have his gear with him even when only going for a look or to make a photograph. All of a sudden I remembered that in the saddle bag of my bike I carried a complete float tackle on a winder. It did not take long to fix this rather stout stuff to an ordinary pole and, to cut the story short, after the keeper had given me some bread, I hooked a small fish within two minutes of my wetting the line. About 4 or 5lb, he made plenty of noise on the 10 foot long line and in the end, when nearly worn out and still in the thickest of reeds, the barb pulled through his upper lip and while still hooked, he managed to attach the barb to a reedstem. Only he had no breath left to, with one movement of his tail, break free. I looked on for a few seconds and then decided to get a boat and free both the fish and my hook. I had had a taste of it and I did not want to lose this, my only way of getting carp at this moment. I could have stepped into the water, but I did not want to get my trousers and footwear all wet because of this small fellow. I was not really fishing anyhow, so I fetched a boat and pushed right through everything - not without some trouble for those reeds were rather massive. I freed the hook and let the carp go, after which I got out again and brought back the boat. I walked around to where I had shoved the pole and line ashore and I don't know what made me do it, but I baited up again and dropped a fresh bit of breadbait in exactly the same place. And within ten minutes I had another bite and in exactly the same way I had another carp of roughly the same size. The third one was somewhat bigger, though I was learning all the time and kept the fish on a shorter line. I had weighed up the breaking strain by then; this one, too, asked for a boat. Here I must add that, after having hooked the fish and after having the fish sort of attach themselves to the reeds, I just put down the rod, exhausted as they were. It must have taken me at least five minutes to get the boat to the spot, yet in the meantime they seemed not to have moved a fin.

I did not consider this a very sporting way of catching carp at all, yet when I heard no fish had been taken by any one angler that very morning, I did feel a little pleased with myself, even if it had been as easy as kiss-your-hand and the carp only small fish really.

We all know, I think, the way large trout and pike select a hidey-hole for themselves from which they, at certain times only, move after food. In all lakes I have in these years visited, public and private alike, I have found many carp do the very same thing and more specially, when these are present, under and in between the roots of a tree standing at the water's edge. And, most curious, I have found they leave their hideout nearly always only in the very late afternoon. In different waters I have found the time roughly to correspond, about the last hour before sunset to half an hour before dark. Just like having a little swim around and a bite to eat before turning in. Yet at the same time in the same water, other carp seem to be moving about like we may have been expecting, while these fellows lay quietly under the slightly hol-lowed-out bank in between their beloved roots. The reader may be assured it is as I state, for I have been in a position several times to observe them closely and I have given some of these fish, which I could clearly discern, nicknames. Some of them, not especially very large fish, I have, after I had caught a couple of these 'cave-dwellers' as I call them, left unfished for and therefore not told other anglers about their presence.

I have had much more fun going to have a look at them from time to time than I would have had pulling them out. My attention was first drawn to them one evening when I was fishing for tench in a very still and shallow water where I had seated myself not far from a small tree. It was midsummer and not yet eight in the evening when I heard some repeated noises, like a baby makes when drinking. I waited for a short time and made sure the noise came from underneath the tree; and I went on all fours to investigate. The tall grass hid me well enough even though I had to go right on my stomach, when nearing the edge, to be sure it was a carp sucking at the moss-covered half-submerged roots. The sight of the fish was plenty reason for me to go back and get my rod. I carefully cast my bait right on the other side of the tree as close to the carp as possible and threw in some breadcrumbs to attract his attention to the paste on my float-ledgered hook. Of course, the first time he took me quite unawares, for I had been watching some terns for a second or two. The moment I struck far too much line was drawn off my reel already, and it was only a simple thing to have me tied up to the roots. I did not see the fish at this same station again for quite a few weeks, but in the meantime I had been having similar looks at a great number of trees in the neighbourhood and I had discovered a nice number of carp this way. Soon I had caught a couple of them, and it was then that I began to take more proper notice of the time I had taken them. Never did I get one in the early morning hours or afternoon, which last may well be understood. But the hour past sunset was definitely not as productive as the hour before, a fact which seemed rather surprising to me and it is that still, because I have in nearly all other circumstances come to regard the time around dusk as the very best period of the day. (It should be stated that, in Holland, no night fishing is allowed.) I could not grasp this for a long time, and as I am not quickly satisfied, I went around trying to collect evidence of this evening walk. I got it in the end when I came to a shallow water with a large amount of reed-growth. Here I searched till I found a root-dweller. And because of the thick reeds the fish could not leave his lair without moving up their stems so much it was child's work to follow the way he swam. Always around the same time away from sunset (this is not the same as at exactly the same hour) the fish left and always moved along the same pathways and never more than 8 or 9 yards from the tree, from which the carp was never away for more than half an hour. I know this for certain, for after I had discovered about which time of the day he was to leave I lay down on my stomach and watched him go and come and I timed his outings many a time. One would be inclined to think that such a fish would go short of food, for half an hour isn't much time in which to eat enough vitamins or fattening food. Yet they seemed just in as good a condition as any fish I had ever seen. Again I started wondering whether I was rightly sure my observations had been completed. I spent more hours still and even so I could not detect anything else. After I had landed another fish I hit on an entirely new idea: and straightaway I felt I had something there. I therefore went to a private lake where a boat can be had and poled across its water from the rather bare bank to a spot where several stunted trees grew, mostly slanting over the water. I must state that here the bank is not higher than l foot above the surface and that the soil is marshy and spongy - it vibrates heavily when one tries to walk on it. I stopped the boat just outside about in the middle of the 20 yards of bank occupied by these trees. With the long pole I groped and pushed into the bank under the surface in between the roots. Nearly the whole length of the pole, certainly more than 8 feet, disappeared under the hollow bank. This is where big carp found a good resting place and where many a hook could be fastened nicely to the roots. What I want to point out, however, is the puzzle how this bank, strongly reinforced by the tree roots against the waves of any hard winds which would otherwise have forced it back, became undermined. At first I thought this must have been done by the elements. But afterwards I found the same symptoms where the wind and the waves could not possibly have done the damage, for in spots the waves have only perhaps a 'run' of 20 or 30 yards from the other bank of a really small pond. And I believe it is the fish which make such a bank hollow by at first just seeking the shadow of a tree, all the while digging into the soil for food and washing away the loose rubbish by the wash of their fins and tails. In this way these undermined banks must be made in places where neither the waves nor the current of the water has a chance. Not only do the fish have a very difficult-to-get-at hide-out, also they are able by their constant digging into the bank, which no angler can possibly observe, to keep themselves in a much better condition than would be held probable by the fisher-man. Once a lake possesses a few of such really large tackle smash holes, it will, I think, never be without large carp.

Alfred Mackrill's Grand Carp

Anon.

The largest carp I ever heard of as being taken with rod and line in the Thames was caught in Walton Deeps on the 14th of March, 1882 by that clever angler, Mr Alfred Mackrill, who thus descries his fight with his grand fish - taken, it must be remembered, in running water, on fine tackle, which means that the slightest mistake on the part of the angler would lose the fish:

'I was fishing for bream with a 14oz rod, a running line of plaited silk about the thickness of cotton, a fine gut ledger trace, and a No. 5 round-bend hook mounted on very fine gut. Old George had baited the hook with one of the largest brandlings I ever saw, quite five inches long. Suddenly out went the line, forty yards at least right into the river, which was running about two miles an hour. By a twist of the rod I turned the fish, which went right away again, then straight into the hole under the bushes. Now came the struggle. I had to fairly lie down in the bottom of the punt to keep the top of the rod level with the water. This was a very anxious time - I had to hold the winch in my hand, and let out six inches at a time with a strain on the winch. The fish was fairly under the boughs. I then had to hold on and trust to the tackle. The little rod bent like the letter U; it was a fair case of 'Pull devil, pull baker.' I must here remark this was the last day of the fishing season, and the occupants of several punts paid me a visit to see the performance. The tackle stood the strain with the assistance of the rod. I gave a little turn of the wrist, and the fish dashed off for the other side of the river. So I let him go, and felt sure I should, if careful, succeed. Back he came for the punt, went right under, and I had to lie down and put out my rod nearly two feet into the water, round the end of the punt to clear, then out went the fish into the middle of the river, back again for the ryepeck. Now I thought it was all up. Old George put out his landing-net. I did not use profane language, but I told him in plain English to keep away. This duel lasted for fifty-five minutes. I managed by playing the fish on the winch to fairly kill it, and it floated on the top lifeless. Old George placed the landing-net in the water, and I drew the fish over with the line humming like a harp-string. After showing the spectators the carp, which Old George held up by the gills, and receiving an ovation from the assembled anglers, it was dropped into the well of the punt. I tried to fish again, but it was useless, my arm shook like a man suffering from palsy. We started for home. On the bank, just in front of the Swan Hotel, we found a crowd waiting to see the 'Great Thames Carp', which weighed 12½lb.'

Overbeck's Monster

Horace Hutchinson

Mr Overbeck gives us an account of a tremendous fight he had with a monster carp, which he hooked on his 20-foot salmon rod at 11am, and which he played until 4.30pm, and then lost!

'It was, he says, nearly eleven when my reel gave a sudden violent rush, and the line hissed madly through the water faster than I could run on dry land. I was into one, and possibly a good one, and good luck too, for he was on my 20-foot salmon rod, with which I can lift a fish far off.

But this one - oh, dear me, no! not a bit of it; not a sign could I get of him, now nearly 100 yards off. Suddenly I noticed that my line was nearly all gone, and all hopes of turning him also, so I bit off the line of a neighbouring rod and my own tackle during a lull, and rapidly changing reels knotted both ends, and before the fish could guess I had another 100 yards for him. A friend holding my rod, I got into my long waders (up to my neck) and in I went through the forest of bulrushes that hid us from the fish into one foot of mud and the same of water. There was my whale seventy yards off now, with my line attached as if nailed to a steamer, with far less hopes of ever coming to a landing stage. How he tugged and sailed to and fro, no signs of his size being possible, his nearest approach within an hour being perhaps fifty yards. Twelve o'clock, ditto; by this time I admired, but no longer loved, my fish. I was now in thick, sticky, slimy, black, very foul-smelling mud up to the knees, and found it difficult to stand or change feet. I had no boots or shoes on my waders, and when I did reach the bottom of the shivering sludge I was firmly glued upon a sharp chalky bottom, with tender feet. Above this mud was two feet of water, for I was right out in the pond by this time. Excitement had given way to philosophy; wild bets were exchanged as to his weight, the boy's estimate being something over a hundredweight, but then he had to be loyal, for I was his master. Tobacco smoke cooled the fumes of excitement, and silence reigned at 1pm, for we (and poor me) were hungry. And, Great Scot! wasn't I tired too – I now respected my fish – and still the same monotonous to and fro went on. Perhaps when about two o'clock came, upon earnest requests to put more force on, although my rod was bent double and I dared not risk another ounce, I managed to rise him and turn him over.

I have never seen such a fish in my life - his belly seemed to be nearly a foot deep - and that was the only time we saw him. Loyal sportsmen as we were, no fish no grub, and still we hungered! At three he started to burrow down into the mud; then I blessed the fish, and down, down he went, up again, shorter runs, although still too deep to see and too heavy to lift. I then gave the rod over to a friend, and proceeded up the pond side to mend, under water, bail out, and bring over the old punt. This I managed with oilcloth, tacks, and much tact, to do, bailed it out (now wet through) - I, not the boat - and brought it down the pond. It was then nearly half-past four, and my friend shouted out that it had buried itself; then I blessed the fish more forcibly still, and resolved to 'elevate' it a little more yet, when, as I came near, a sudden noise of volcanic energy resounded throughout the woods as the gut came in gently by itself, at last sawn through, and I came out!

Then we had dinner, and I masticated my food instead of biting my lips. I even then felt ready to dig for him with a spade if I had only known exactly where to dig.

Among the Carp

G. Christopher Davies

The window of our bedroom was left open, and the cool night air, fresh from the rain-wet woods, filled the chamber, so that our sleep was healthy, and therefore dreamless and light. At four o'clock the next morning we were broad awake, and looking out westward over the fair country. The fields were silver-grey with innumerable rain-drops, but the clouds had gone away to the northward, and a grey-blue sky and hazy weathergleam foretold the coming of a hot day. The breeze came in gentle puffs, bringing to one's nostrils the fragrance of the roses, and the heavier and richer odour of the meadow-sweet, which, in the meadow yonder, shook its cream-white clusters over the ripening hay. The sparrows twittered and chirruped with great industry on the eaves, and the starlings preened themselves on the dovecote.

About two hundred yards from the house was a pool, small in size and shallow, but full of carp, which were at all times most difficult to catch. One side of the pool was bounded by the lane, and on the other was a field containing a savage white bull, the terror of all trespassing anglers. All day long the country urchins sat on the lane side of the pool and fished for small carp of two or three inches in length, and their persistent efforts effectually frightened the bigger fish, so that none could be caught on ordinary occasions. The previous evening, a younger brother named Herbert, a lad of seventeen, had arranged with us that we should try for them early in the morning, and hence it was that we dressed hastily and 'anyhow' (oh, the delight of being able to dress 'anyhow!'), and left our room with the intention of waking Herbert. Our quarters were in a portion of the house separated from the rest of the house by a distinct staircase and doors, and when past these, we had no clear idea where his room lay. So we went prospecting, creeping stealthily with stockinged feet, lest we should rouse the house, and yet it seemed to us that every oaken plank we stepped upon had a loud and distinctive creak. Listening at one door we heard a dual sound of breathing; at another, there was no sound at all. While standing uncertain, a third door opened, and out came Master Herbert, ready for the fray. Our first visit was to the larder for it is a golden rule never to commence the day upon an empty stomach.

We were soon at the pool, on the surface of which thin wisps and veils of mist still slumbered. A heron stood in the marginal weeds, and was so incredulous of visitors so early, that he blinked and blinked his sleepy eyes at us in wonder, and only arose when we were within ten yards of him. Our hooks were baited with red worms, and our lines were dropped quietly into the water, supported by the tiniest floats. While we waited and watched for the first bite, we drew in huge draughts of the exhilarating morning air, with an additional zest, because we knew that the day would turn out scorching hot. All around was very quiet and still, and we noticed what a different nature charac- terises the stillness of the morning and that of the night. In both, the silence is equally profound away from the houses; but while at night the quiet is in accordance with the dying day and the darkness, in the morning it is in keen contrast with the quivering brightness, the intoxicating freshness, and the vigour which impels to action.

A float moves a little, then dips slightly, and then lies still, as if no fish had touched the bait. Patience! he is at it still. Now it slides away with quickening pace, and then dips under water, towards a tree root. Strike, and hold him by the head! Give him the butt, for he is in dangerous proximity to the sunken branches. Now lead him into the rushes. He is landed, a fine carp of two pounds weight.

So we went on, now one and then the other hooking a fish, until ten fine carp lay on the bank. The mists arose from the water, the pearls vanished from the meadow-grasses, the insect hum grew louder, and the thrushes sang in the poplars, the sky brightened into its clearest blue – and the fish ceased biting. It was seven o'clock, and we had not done badly, yet, like Oliver, we asked for more and were admonished. The tiny sprats of carp commenced biting vigorously, and the frequent dips of our floats inspired us with delusive hopes. We had been fishing from the lane, but seeing that the bull was feeding quietly in a far corner of the field with his head turned away from us, we climbed over the gate and went on with our fishing. Presently we heard a tramp and a bellow, and lo! there was the bull close upon us and charging valiantly. One of us scrambled headlong over the gate, just in time to dispense with the bull's assistance, and the other, whose line was fast in a root at this inopportune moment, jumped waist-deep into the pool, and waded out at the other side. Our fishing was at an end, and, laughing heartily, we gathered up our spoil and departed.

The Gipsy was still sleeping the sleep of the just, and when she was awakened she was very incredulous of our early rising, seeing that in the town we were always loath to get up in the mornings.

The heat grew sultry and oppressive; the men laboured mechanically in the hay-fields, the fly-catchers which had been industriously foraging from their stations on the standard-roses, grew tired and quiet. A small black cloud came from over the Wrekin, the rounded crest of which stood out clear and sunny beneath it. Speedily the heavens were overcast, and a dark, eerie stillness reigned over the landscape. The forked lightning flashed whitely down to the earth, and redly back again to the clouds; the heavens opened, and a deluge of rain descended that drove us all indoors.

From the shelter of the verandah we watched the storm, which awed the most careless of us by its grandeur. The three tall poplars waved white against the gloomy canopy, and trembled under the pealing and crashing of the thunder. The rain beat savagely upon the complaining branches, and sprang up again in angry jets from the pools. The birds sat quailing in their nests, or skulked low down in the hedges. The flycatcher sitting on her nest in the verandah let us touch her without moving; she was so fearful of the tempest that she seemed to be glad of our company and protection. Hay-making was suspended. The hay already cut had been gathered hastily into cocks, and would not take much harm; but it was feared that the wheat would be much beaten down by the weight of the rain.

When the fierceness of the tempest had passed away, a steady rain set in, hiding not only the hills, but the near woods in its 'mournful fringe'. At night it grew finer, and we ventured out on the lawn with a lantern to pick up the worms which we imagined would, after rain, be crawling about in great numbers. To our astonishment there were none; the heavy rain had apparently frightened them, so that they had sunk deeper in the earth; for while gentle rain will bring them out in great numbers, 'heavy wet' does not agree with them, but drives them deeper in.

We were rather puzzled to know how we should obtain bait for the morrow, until we stumbled against an old box in which the gardener had stored some rich mould for his flower-pots. Upon emptying this we found great numbers of capital redworms. To make assurance doubly sure, we got some gunpowder, and

making a big 'devil', sallied forth and stormed a wasps'
nest in an adjoining lane.

The morning broke with a bright blue sky, across
which the clouds were being rapidly driven by a
strong breeze from the south-east. It was not the best
of days for carp fishing, but we started, driving to the
town, and then stoutly facing the five mile walk uphill
to the pool. Over meadow, through brake, through
brier, over streams, and up crags, we pushed our way,
passing well-remembered spots which had known no
change, and brought back to us scenes of our happy
boyhood with startling clearness. The jay flew chat-
tering through the wood as of old, the pheasant
flustered, and the rabbit scuttled. On the same bank
grew the same thick growth of Blechnum ferns, the
redstart built in the same hole of the grey stone wall,
and everything was so fresh and beautiful with the old
freshness and beauty, that we began to believe that we
also had not changed; and by the time we reached the
lovely pool on the hilltop, we were prepared to enjoy
ourselves with the old keenness, and it seemed just as
if it were a Saturday half-holiday years ago.

There were three of us - the writer, his young
brother Herbert, and one whom we will call Senior -
full of quips and cranks and merry jests, complaining
loudly of the steepness and difficulty of the way, and

stopping very often to gather the wild strawberries which grew in remarkable profusion all the way, peeping with timid blushes from their sheltering, half-concealing leaves. Herbert was but seventeen - a tall, pleasant lad, clever and thoughtful beyond his years, and with a most mad propensity for punning; and the worst of it was that his puns were so apt, and uttered with such quaint gravity, that one was compelled to laugh at them.

Before us lay the pool in its sheltered hollow, reed surrounded, with inner belts of rushes and the smooth water horse-tail; its surface intersected with waterhens and coots, a heron in the shallows, and wild ducks playing on an iris-island. The very water was greenish in colour, and then it had a background of alders, and willows, and black fir-forest.

Our rods were soon together; but an unforeseen difficulty arose. The water of the pool was unusually high, and had flooded the belt of willows around, covering the few standing-places there had ever been. It was far too cold to wade, and it really seemed as if we could not get at the pool to fish it. At the only open space it was too shallow. At last we discovered a spot at the lee-side of the pool, where, by breaking down the branches of the dwarf willows, and placing a line of stepping-stones, we could just make room for one to stand. Even then there was not sufficient room to swing the rod backwards for a throw-out, and the wind was so strong that it was difficult to throw in its teeth.

Herbert had brought with him a salmon rod, which had been given to him, and which he had never before used. Knowing the usual difficulty of reaching out, he had wisely brought it with him, and he was able to commence fishing at once - his float lying twenty feet beyond ours, which reposed uncomfortably just outside the rushes. While we were debating what we should do, Herbert's float moved away through the dancing ripples with a most decisive bite. He struck, and the carp, firmly hooked, dashed out towards the centre of the pool, taking out line like a salmon, and making the splendid rod bend and spring delightfully. After taking out fully fifty yards of line, he allowed himself to be turned, and came zigzagging back with sullen resistance, until he was close into the rushes, and then he proceeded to dash backwards and forwards, catching up both our lines, which were still in the water, and getting them into a pretty tangle. Herbert played him very steadily, though he was much excited, and at last he led him up a sort of drain, and we closed in behind him and lifted him out - a splendid fish of 6lb in weight.

Leaving Herbert to re-bait, we rushed about seeking some means of getting at the pool. Not far off was a small cottage, which, upon examination, we found to be uninhabited. The garden presented a sad appearance, currant and gooseberry bushes running wild, and the beds overgrown with weeds. The door of the cottage was open, and we conceived and put into execution a capital idea. We took the door off its hinges, and collected a quantity of loose bricks. Transporting these to the pool, we speedily constructed a platform on which there was just room for the three of us to stand.

We had no lack of bites. Barely five minutes passed without one or other of us having a bite. The pool, in all probability, had not been fished for some years, and the carp were not shy. But we missed a great many. Our floats were necessarily very close together, as we were fishing in a small bay; and when the float began to slide away with the peculiar motion of the carp-bite, if we struck too soon we missed the fish to a certainty, and if we gave it the proper time it entangled us with our neighbour's lines, and spoilt the chance for a time. Herbert had the most bites, as his bait was the farthest out, and he caught the most fish. Then, whenever a fish was struck by one of us, the others had to 'up stick' and away, to give room for the carp to dash about in, and to aid in their landing. It was excessively inconvenient, but excellent fun, and a very novel position. For a time we had very good sport, catching fish of 2 to 4lb in weight, but none so big as the first one. Then they ceased biting; and no wonder, for the bay had been thoroughly disturbed, and the writer began to speculate if he could not find fresh fields and pastures new. At the windward side of the pool it was far too shallow to fish it from the bank, but a line of rickety posts and rails ran out into the pool, enclosing a space where the cattle were allowed to drink and bathe. As this part of the pool was sheltered from the wind by the trees and hillside, it was calm and smooth, and rippled only by the back fins of the huge carp sailing about. The writer thought he would scramble out upon these rails, and he proceeded to do so. As he went to the shore-end of the rails, he saw many large carp with their noses to the bank, in only six inches of water. They were grubbing away in the mud in search of food, but when he placed his bait at their very noses they took no notice of it, save to scurry away with a huge wave and upheaval of mud.

It was very ticklish work scrambling along the rotten rails, but at last he gained the farthest point, and there, with some two feet of water and some six feet of mud below him, he balanced himself on a rail an inch wide and fished for carp. Grave misgivings crossed his mind as to how he should land the fish when he hooked them: but he was spared the risk. Great carp of 10lb weight came wallowing at his very feet, gasping and sucking with their round fleshy mouths, and turning away from the worm which was all but put down their very throats. It was very tantalising to see such big fellows utterly impervious to his blandishments, and he could not forbear striking at one of them with the butt-end of his rod, seriously endangering thereby his seat upon the rail. Not a bite did he get. He was out of the wind, and the sun blazed hotly upon his back. The rail was *cutting*, very; and he saw that his companions were again catching fish. So he crept back again and rejoined them.

During another lull in the biting we came off our platform to get some lunch and stretch our legs a little, laying our rods down to fish for themselves, Herbert being told off to keep an eye upon them. Suddenly he rushed forward, exclaiming, "I have a bite!" and we watched him take up his rod and play a large fish. While he was doing so another float had disappeared without our knowledge, and a 'scurr' of a reel and a splash in the water told us that a rod had disappeared into the pool. It dived clean out of sight, and the first we saw of it again was its top bobbing up full sixty yards out. The reel kept the butt-end under, and the top just emerged now and then as the fish ceased to pull for an instant. It was *our* rod - plague upon the pronouns! - not the plural 'our', but the singular 'our' of the author (if we use 'I', we may be accused of egotism); so 'we', not wishing to lose a valuable rod, rapidly undressed and plunged into the pool. We swam after the rod, and, after following it full a hundred and fifty yards, we lost sight of it. Just then the butt-end struck against our legs, and, diving down, we seized it. There were quite forty yards of line out, and the fish was still on. Now commenced a most exciting struggle. Holding the rod in one hand, we swam with the other, and, not without some trouble, we landed ourselves, and eventually the fish, which was 3lb in weight.

A goodly heap of fish lay side by side upon the grass - seventeen in number, and all good-sized ones. There were quite as many as we could carry, so we left off fishing and rambled about gathering wild strawberries, chasing conies, seeking for young wood-pigeons wherewith to make a pie, and generally behaving ourselves in a very silly, boyish, yet happy way. In truth, the youngest of us was by far the sedatest, and looked down with calm superiority upon our elderly frolics.

A great part of the wood had been cut down since the old times, so that we could see away over a forest of foxglove to the wild Welsh hills. Silent and still they lay in the swift-chasing sunshine and shadow. Their lower sides were green with irregularly mapped-out fields, and dotted with lonely farm-houses, from which the smoke crept lazily upwards, or whirled downwards before a sudden gust of wind. The sheep were so distant and small that their motions were not observable, and they gave no life to the view, so that as far as the eye could see all was still and lonely. A tiny village, clustered round an ancient church, seemed at that distance dead and deserted.

The hilltops arrested the flying clouds that broke against them, and streamed up the glens like rivers with an upwards current. The rounded outlines of the nearer hills changed in the distance to the bluff crags and bold projections of the Snowdon mountains. Over the valley the raven floated from his nest on the inaccessible cliff, and his shadow fell on the sunny fields below. The ordered confusion, the solidity and grandeur of the many hills, and the loveliness of their intersecting glens, spoke of half-savage wildness and half-barbaric freedom; yet the denizens of those sequestered farms held themselves but as serfs in bondage to a rich landowner. They claimed the independence of the Cymri, yet bowed down slavishly to the will of their landlord - and why? Because they must live, and poverty falls with the snow in these wild hill villages, and springs up with the stones in their ploughed fields - and as poverty teaches so do they learn. So that, to him who looks under the surface, the fair freshness of the hill country is too often but a painful foil to the narrow and straitened life beneath.

We had but to turn around, and there before us, for mile on mile, stretched the greater portion of four fine counties: rich plains, massy woods, silver winding streams, and landmark hills such as the Wrekin, the Breidden, Hawkstone, Longmynd, and others. There peace and plenty reigned; and comfortable homesteads, and well-filled stackyards, spoke to the gold that came from the bosom of the earth.

Around us the wind sighed loudly in the fir-trees, and the ripples washed among the reeds. There was no sound of man or domestic animal - nothing save our own voices, and the croak of the coots, and cackle of wild-ducks, and noises in the wood which were hard to assign to their natural causes. The excitement of the sport being over, the place seemed uncanny, and we quickly divided our spoil into three bundles and started homewards. We were heavily laden, and long ere the five miles were passed we were thoroughly fagged. The waggonette was waiting for us, and the Gipsy was there too. "So you have caught some fish at last!" she cries; "I am glad to see that you *can* catch them sometimes." She is very incredulous, is the Gipsy, about our piscatory feats.

A Carp in the Night

Gerry Berth Jones

Dagenham is a flooded gravel pit of some ten acres. It is shallow over most of its area with a carpet of silk-weed growing to a height of three to five inches over most of its bottom. Banks are high and steep and uncomfortable for the angler who wishes to stay quiet and concealed.

We elected to fish from the east bank so that we should have the stiff breeze in our faces, which I am certain is of great importance. Reason for this comes later.

We had a clear bank to our left and a dreadful tangle of willows coming right down to the water's edge 40 yards to the right hand. Our tackle included a special No. 2 hook designed by the Carp Catchers' Club.

My second baited swim lay 30 yards to my left but only six feet from the bank because I am so sure that carp come very close inshore at night to grub about the margins of the lake on the windward side, to avail themselves of grazing ground that would be too dangerous by daylight, and also for the many scraps that follow the wind-made surface currents.

Derek and I settled to fish in utter discomfort. Rain lashed about us in squally showers.

We fished on through the darkness, talking in low whispers - mostly about carp fishing technique. Derek preferred to use the accepted Dagenham rig, which is simply a running lead stopped five inches or so from the hook, so that the crust (a very large piece) is allowed to rise to the top of the five-inch layer of silkweed.

Thus suspended, the crust bait is visible to cruising carp. This is fine - in daylight. But carp, we believe, cannot see any more than we can by night, so for this reason I used plain breadpaste on one rig (the one near the bank) and balanced paste and crust on the other.

Carp are surely more accustomed to finding the food on the bottom amongst this silkweed and we must give them credit for being able to find it there.

At precisely five minutes past two in the morning a carp found mine! The silver paper which was folded over my line between bottom rings and free open spool began to move off slowly – it was the outfit lying close to the left bank.

It crept upwards in the darkness and jammed against the butt-ring; the line rustled through unchecked. A pause, a pounding heart, a lightning check on my tackle, then in went the pick-up and I struck.

I at once knew that I had hooked a heavy fish. It ran for the centre of the lake in great haste with a headlong dash, the power of which astonished me.

Quickly I clambered up the sheer bank to gain a better control of the situation. Derek switched on the big torch and together we walked down the bank to our left to follow the fish although he was now over 80 yards from the bank.

Fifty yards from where our fish was first hooked, Derek dropped once again down to water level and kept the powerful beam upon the taut singing line and bucking rod.

After a dogged fight of some 15 minutes which went decidedly in favour of the fish, I began to gain several yards of line with a long pumping action.

After the twentieth minute of battle I became a little curious to see my fish. It is always a dangerous procedure to bring a lively fish to the surface, especially if he is a big carp.

Derek warned me with wise words to treat him

with respect, and I should have done. But he was below me now, not 20 feet from the bank and sulking. I eased him off the bottom gently; yard by yard he came up for all the world to me like a sack of wet sand.

Faintly from the dark water out in front came a 'plop'. I asked Derek to direct the beam in that direction and there lay motionless a huge black shape with back fin, shark-like, cutting the surface.

The carp then swam slowly and majestically by us and as his great flank caught the beam he was transformed into a bar of glittering gold. Such a spectacle I shall never forget.

Derek's sharp remarks regarding my dangerous tactics, were drowned in a thunderous, gigantic swirl as the fish, regaining his senses, turned head down and lashed his tail in fury, sending spray sparkling into the torchlight and causing the fixed-spool reel to scream like a scalded cat. Eighty yards were gone from the spool in a twinkling, yet almost as quickly retrieved; he was surely beginning to tire now.

Thirty minutes now, and my specially made outsize landing-net was placed in readiness in the very capable hands of Derek Davenport. At this point the fish made a brisk run inshore 15 feet from where we stood heading for a clump of loosely growing reedmace.

Derek picked up some flint stones from the water's edge and threw them at the reeds. This disturbance had the desired effect; the carp turned and headed out towards midwater.

At thirty-three minutes I was more forceful. With rod held high I walked three paces to the rear to bring him, bewildered, over the waiting mesh. Derek needed no second chance. He did a fine job. The words came to me, "OK, he's yours!"

I felt a tremendous feeling of relief. But then, as Derek took the mesh into his grasp to lift, it began to break under the strain. I laid the rod down upon the wet grass at my feet and hurriedly jumped down the bank. Together we heaved and rolled the great bulk away out of danger where the hook almost fell out!

Next morning we took the fish to the club house to be officially weighed. Two separate scale weighings produced 23 pounds 10 ounces exactly. It was entered in the club book and I proudly signed.

We then took the carp to the water's edge, and, with a curious feeling of regret and pleasure, I saw my carp swim majestically away to dissolve as a shadow into the sunlit depths of Dagenham lake.

The Susceptible Carp

J. H. Keene

The carp is a fish very susceptible of electrical impressions. Of this I have repeatedly convinced myself by insulating a convenient receptacle containing carp, and passing a charge of electricity through the water. Although previously still, and apparently asleep, the immediate excitement caused by the shock it is impossible to describe, whilst the process of filling a glass globe, containing these fish, with electricity, as one would a Leyden jar, has produced in the fish a state of uncontrollable agitation painful to witness. There is no doubt that earth currents influence other fish - especially trout - in an analogous manner; and from water being a superior conductor of the electric fluid to air, I infer that the effect of atmospheric changes on fish are, in proportion, more marked than the same on the human being. We all know how much the weather has to do with the general balance of our own healths.

We are informed in the *Whole Art of Fishing*, 1719, that the 'carp is a stately and subtle fish, called the fresh-water fox and queen of rivers' - queen of rivers, I suppose, on somewhat the same principle as that on which St Ambrose terms the grayling 'the flower of fishes'. In Heraldry, Randle Holme, in his marvellous collection of knowledge, *The Academy of Armory,* informs us the carp indicates 'hospitality, and denotes food and nourishment from the bearer to those in need'. The associations of carp history are therefore redolent of salutary lessons and good qualities, truly suggesting generally the sacred ideal of being wise as a serpent and harmless as a dove.

The date of the introduction of this fish into England is not quite satisfactorily proved. The old rhyme in Sir Richard Baker's *Chronicle*:

Hops and turkeys, carps and beer,
Came into England all in a year

- is of course not correct. Leonard Mascal asserts that he introduced them, and Walton speaks of the circumstance as follows: 'It is said they were brought hither by one Mr Mascal, a gentleman that then lived in Plumstead, in Essex.' This assertion is, however, not true, for in 1496 Dame Berners says, 'There be but few in Englonde,' which is of course equivalent to saying there were some, but not many. Mr Manley, in the work before quoted, says they were probably imported from Persia and naturalised in the fourteenth century, but does not give his authority - a grave omission. Still, one may safely assume that the carp was a foreign importation about that time. It was introduced into Sweden in 1560, and has since become perfectly naturalised there.

Shakespeare mentions it (*Hamlet*, Act 2, Scene 1), in Polonius' advice to his son, and both Massinger and Ben Jonson refer to the tongues of carps as eatables.

The artfulness of this fish is indeed remarkable. More than one writer has paid a tribute to this quality. Duncombe translates Vaniere's oft quoted eulogium in a capitally vigorous style:

Of all the fish that swim the watery weed,
Not one in cunning can the carp exceed.
She oft will dive
Beneath the net, and not alone contrive
Means for her own escape, but pity take
On all her hapless brethren of the lake;
For rising, with her back she lifts the snares,
And frees the captive with officious cares;
The little fry in safety swim away,
And disappoint the nets of their expected prey.

Another and more amusing poetical commemoration of the craft of the carp has been extracted from the *Censura Literaria,*and published by Mr Pinkerton. I have not space for more than a stanza or two. It is entitled *The Cunning Carp and the Contented Knight.* To the tune of St George and the Dragon:

Within the wood a virgin ash
Had twenty summers seen.
The elves and fairies marked it oft,
As they tripped it on the green;
But the woodman cut it with his axe,
He cruelly felled it down,
A rod to make for the Knight of the Lake,
A Knight of no renown.
Turn and taper it round, turner,
Turn and taper round,
For my line is of the grey palfrey's tail,
And it is slender and sound.

St George he was for England,
St Dennis he was for France.
St Patrick taught the Irishman
To tune the merry harp.
At the bottom of the slimy pool
There lurks a crafty carp;
Were he at the bottom of my line,

How merrily he would dance.

Moulded and mixed is the magic mass,
The sun is below the hill;
O'er the dark water flits the bat,
Hoarse sounds the murm'ring rill;
Slowly bends the willow's bough
To the beetle's sullen tune;
And grim and red is the angry head
Of the archer in the moon.
Softly, softly, spread the spell,
Softly spread it around;
But name not the magic mixture
To mortal that breathes on ground.

St George, etc.

The Knight having risen at sunrise and duly arranged his tackle, begins to fish – but the 'magic mass' is ineffectual.

The carp peeped out from his reedy bed,
And forth he slyly crept;
But he liked not the look, for he saw the black hook,
So he turned his tail and slept.
There is a flower grows in the field,
They call it marigold-a,

And that which one fish would not take
Another surely wold-a.
And the Knight had read in the books of the dead,
So the Knight did not repine,
For they that cannot get carp, sir,
On tench may very well dine.

St George, etc.

But it was all of no use. The 'sly tenant of the pool' was too old to be tempted into an indiscretion so flagrant.

Then up spoke the lord of Penbury's board,
Well skilled in musical lore,
And he swore by himself, though cunning the elf,
He would charm him and draw him ashore.
The middle of day he chose for the play,
And he fiddled as in went the line,
But the carp kept his head in the reedy bed,
He chose not to dance nor to dine.
"I prithee come dance me a reel, carp,
I prithee come dance me a reel."
"I thank you, my lord, I've no tart for your board,
You'd much better play to the eel."

St George, etc

A Taste of the Dairymaid

George Brennand

I have little doubt that that rare species of *Piscicidus*, the Giant Carpers, represent the true aristocracy of Waltonia, for consider these things:

Their craft is in direct descent from the art of the Master himself; infinite patience is theirs and an infinite virtuosity in the deception of the most cunning of fish and in the playing of corpulent monsters of fifteen pounds and twenty pounds on tackle almost as fine as the Roach Man's and quite as delicate as any used by the Dun Worshippers. Add to this the painfully acquired knowledge necessary to achieve even one bite and this assertion of superiority must appear well sustained.

How truly should their motto be '*Carpe Diem*', for does not this remarkable species contrive to wait, in cunning 'hides' or in small bivouac tents, for hours and days and maybe weeks, for that fleeting moment when, far down below the lily-pads, some great and priest-like fish takes just one small potato or a pear-shaped bait of kneaded cheese and bread? True denizens of Arcadia are those rare and happy types and sojourners amid immemorial things, on the margins of still meres, and among the shadows of historic oaks; and how like some lordly abbot of an older England is the noble carp himself. How truly did Richard Frank of the seventeenth century write of him: 'The carp is a fish complicated of a moross mixture and a torbid motion . . . Ponds and pools are generally his palaces, where he loves good eating; but seldom or rarely travels far to fetch it . . . All the summer season he bites without dispute, if he likes his commons . . .

Ah, there's the rub – 'if he likes his commons'. And of those same commons let us again quote the honest Frank on the matter of paste for a carp: 'Take fine bean-flower, English honey and poudred sugar, amalgamized or mingled with the yolk of an egg; and if the fat of an heron be superadded to it, it makes it not the worse. Besides, sometimes he loves a taste of the dairy-maid; as at other times he affects the smell of the shambles . . .'

'The taste of the dairy-maid.' What mystic Waltonian rune is this, and as for 'the smell of the shambles', is it not still with us in those dilapidated small shops and those maggot-factories from which we shrank not so long ago?

But after all, is there not a definite 'taste of the dairy-maid' about all these specialized sects of the Coarse Fishers, these Giant Carpers, the Tench Crawlers, the Bleak Spinners and those who frequent the somno-lent Congresses of the Chub? And this subtle art, now, of the Carpers, how far has it not progressed since the days of good Dame Juliana Berners who remarked of the noble carp that 'he is an evyll fysshe to take ... For he is soo stronge enarmyd in the mouthe that there maye noo weke harnays holde hym'. Is there not something completely artistic about the whole approach of the modern Carper? Like the Sea Trouter this species is a night hunter, but how much more subtle and above all quiet. The bivouac tent overlaid with branches and leaves, the false rod of willow that has been left for weeks protruding above the chosen spot, the float made from an oak-twig, the 5x cast and the fine nylon line.

And then the night of nights when the patient Carper replaces the false willow with a long thin rod that is not false, and when below the twig-float there hangs on the gossamer the one small potato or the oblong morsel of special paste.

Softly he crawls into his 'hide'; gently he pulls off

yards of fine nylon and coils it carefully beside the rod-butt; while the more advanced pundits of the Cult have strange and complex devices which ring electric or other types of bell to warn them of the 'run'.

Drowsily the Carper smokes his last pipe and then falls peacefully to sleep . . .

And then all around that silent bivouac the wild things of the night move noiselessly; the hunting fox, the fishing otter and the waddling badger, scent the pipe smoke and the whiff of Man and melt into the warm darkness. In the hollow oak trees a brood of young owls hisses angrily.

And then, and then, far down in the dark lake water a monster opens his great mouth and absorbs the potato. It is a 'run' and the silence is shattered by the shrilling of a little bell.

Yes, lucky indeed is he 'For whom the Bell Tolls'.

But not always is the noble carp taken by these means, for have we not heard rumours of certain adventurous Dun Worshippers who even catch giant carp on crusts of bread? These people, it is said, do indeed cast their bread upon the waters, and the great and wallowing carp will on occasions rise majestically between the lilies and take like any mere two-pounder of the Test.

Soon, no doubt, we shall be introduced to the Bread Fly and there will grow up a new band of purists who will demand that no carp should be caught except by an exact imitation of the 'bread on the water'. And then, God help us, but won't we have the heretic who uses a 'Hovis Fly' or, horrible thought, a 'Sponge-cake Fly?'

The Appeal of the Carp

Michael Shephard

*'The carp is the queen of rivers -
a stately, a good, and a very subtle fish.'*
IZAAK WALTON

If the 'queen of rivers', then, surely, the king of lakes
and pools, for the carp is a fish of still waters, although
good fish are occasionally met with in slow-running
water. Richard Franck recognised this when he wrote,
'The carp is a fish complicated of a moross mixture
and a torpid motion. Ponds and pools are generally
his palaces', and I believe that had it not been for his
Cromwellian conscience he would have crowned him
king of lakes.

There is something about carp fishing which, once
you have experienced it, claims you wholly, just as the
wild goose holds the wild fowler to his exacting chase.
There are fishermen who fish for little else but carp,
and count the world well lost for the sake of a single

thrilling run in a week of nights by the water-side; they think and dream about carp, talk and write about them and agree on two things - that carp, big carp, are not easy to catch and that the catching of one involves more knowledge, more skill and more patience than any other form of fishing and pays a full dividend in return for the efforts made by the fisher-man, for, although torpid in its natural motion as Franck suggested, the fish that feels the hook can move with a power and a speed sufficient to instil a healthy sense of impotence in any angler who is for-tunate to hook a carp on light tackle. The late Hugh Sheringham said that he went in terror of the fish, 'Terror, however, adds a zest to angling, and carp fish-ing has always made a strong appeal to me'. I imagine that all serious carp fishermen must share this 'terror' with awe and respect for the mighty and cunning fish.

I was first attracted to carp fishing when I was at school, for in Hertfordshire ponds you will often find many small carp, and there was such a pond in the garden of one of the masters, who gave me permission to fish. I caught a great number of carp there, but never one of more than a pound in weight, I fished for these little fish because I was a boy at school and it was the only fishing available to me, and because it was fun. Later, a few years before the war, I went carp fishing again, but this time it was because I was drawn to attempt the impossible.

Near my home there was a large, shallow lake - shallow as far as water was concerned but deep in mud and thick with a rather dirty, unhealthy-looking weed. It made me think of the Sargasso Sea. It was a preserve for wild duck, but it also contained big eels and carp. Friends who had fished there day and night testified to the great fish they had seen, but never had a bite. It was impossible, they said, to catch those carp.

One day a fisherman of the town told me that if I could get permission to fish that lake he would show me how the carp could be caught.

I obtained permission, and met my friend one morning at half-past five and drank a cup of tea while he kneaded honey into a stiff bread-paste.

Then we started off in the old car, and reached the water just as the light began to grow from the east beyond the woods and the wild duck flew in over our heads. We embarked in a flat-bottomed boat and poled our way above that murky jungle of weed, preceded by waves which broke the flat, metallic sheen of the surface as large fish moved away from us. It was very exciting to see so much evidence of the fish, but no carp could move fast there without setting up a miniature tidal wave, for the deepest part was not more than four feet and there was only about three feet or less over most of the lake.

Before leaving home my friend Albert had shown me the special tackle we were to use. As he pointed out, in such shallow water we would have to fish a very long line, and that would mean a fairly heavy weight to help in casting; but a heavy weight or a ledger on the bottom would only sink into the ooze and frighten the carp by its resistance when the fish began to move off with the bait. So he had prepared several casts of artificial gut, each nine feet long, with a small treble hook tied to the end. To provide weight for casting and to hold much of the cast off the mud he had made several rough floats from corks, boring a hole in the centre and packing the hole with sheet lead wrapped round inside so that there was room left for the line to pass through and for a wooden plug to hold the float in the desired position on the cast.

As we moved the boat through that sea of weed our rods were up with lines well greased, for we wanted to make as little movement as possible when we reached the scene of action. My rod was a ten-and-a-half-feet sea-trout fly-rod of built cane, chosen for its power to throw a long line and its ability to pick a lot of line off the water quickly; Albert had a very similar rod, but of rather stiffer action. Our reels were

ordinary three and a half-inch centre-pins of the
Nottingham type, and on each there was about one
hundred yards of 8lb breaking strain silk line and
another fifty yards of rather coarser backing. We
reached a place where the weeds gave way to open
water - a space a hundred yards by a hundred and fifty
yards - and gently we moved the boat away from the
tangled mass until we were about thirty yards from it;
there we quietly lowered a weight from each end of
the boat and prepared to fish.

The surface of the lake lay in a flat calm, broken
only by the disturbance of the wild duck, moorhens
and an occasional shoal of small fish. It was said that
the water contained only carp and eels, but I discovered later that there were a lot of small roach there,
although you never saw them in the opaque green
water which I have since learned to associate with
carp. Albert kneaded a piece of honey paste round his
triangle and then showed me how to cast, drawing
about forty yards of line off the reel into the boat and
then, starting at the reel end, coiling it on the water in
front of him. He lifted his rod so that six feet of cast
below the cork swung out gently behind him; he
paused to balance the weight and let another two feet
of the gut down from the rod-top. With his right arm
half bent, he made a strong but even swing with the

rod, continuing the movement until his arm was fully extended in front of him and the baited hook, gut and weighted cork sailed out over the lake, drawing the unresisting line off the water. There was a splash, and as the cork bobbed before settling down, a wave showed that a fish had been disturbed in that place.

Before I cast, Albert decided that we ought to give a worm a trial, so I changed my triangle for a No. 4 hook and baited it with one of the lobworms we had brought with us. My own effort was successful enough and the bait went out smoothly and the line did not snarl up, but it was not as strong as Albert's, and my cork lay on the water about thirty yards from me.

For a while nothing much happened; there was a bit of drift on the lake, and our floating lines bellied round, but not enough to drag the bait, and whenever the line was fully bellied we lifted it to relieve the strain. Away to the left of my cork a big fish rolled in the weeds and then Albert said, "Look . . ." and I saw a tremor on his cork which sent out tiny rings on the surface. So calm was it that even at that distance we could see the slightest movement. The trembling went on and on, occasionally developing into a more determined bob, but moving the cork not at all.

"It's playing with the paste," said Albert, and for a long time after that day we attributed the trembling movement of our floats to carp. Now, however, I believe it was caused by a shoal of small fish, for it went on sometimes for as much as half-an-hour, after which the bait would be brought in for inspection and found to be nibbled right down to the hook. The only movement on my float was the faintest, and caused, I imagine, by the worm, but after twenty minutes I thrilled to see my cork dive under and move a foot or more before it stopped again; a moment later it bobbed violently and began to move off in the other direction, gathering speed until it disappeared. My rod was up, my left hand gathering the line, and as soon as I felt that in another second I should feel the fish I tightened and hooked it.

Where was that vaunted, to-be-feared, exhilarating rush - the long, unmanageable run of the carp? There was a living, moving weight there, to be sure, but it was one which shuddered and shook the rod. After a short run towards the weeds, the wriggling began again, and the surface was broken by the head of a big eel, which fought backwards with all the power of its long, thick body, but was steadily drawn to the boat, netted and despatched before I attempted to remove the hook from its jaw. An eel of 3lb, but for me (who enjoys fishing for big eels) a disappointment.

I put on my triangle and baited with honey paste and tried again, but before I had time to put my rod down, Albert whispered, "I'm off . . ." and I watched his float moving slowly to the right. Bobbing slightly, the cork was drawn along the surface for six feet or more, but never with the appearance of a determined 'take' which would justify striking.

Then the movement stopped, but was followed almost at once by the cork shooting under with an exciting 'plop'. Back on the surface, the cork moved away from us with gathering speed, and the line furrowed the water as it followed; I saw Albert's rod moving gently upwards, the line lifting from the water and gradually tautening until all slack had been regained and then, as the cork was disappearing diagonally below the surface, the rod was brought firmly back over my companion's shoulder, the top bent and the reel tore round, braked by the fisherman's fingers against the rim.

At first I thought that Albert was asking too much of Fortune, but he obviously knew his tackle, and exerted the maximum pressure on the fish so that he checked that terrific run for the weeds much sooner than I would have done and, in fact, subsequently did. Perhaps chastened by its failure to reach the weeds, the fish moved round more slowly, and began to come towards the boat, but as soon as it sensed our presence it turned and rushed across towards my line with such speed that it had travelled twenty yards, and had almost fouled the two lines, before I brought mine in, in the nick of time.

However, control regained, Albert kept up his pressure on the carp, and the fish slowed up, moving round the boat, taking a little line and allowing it to be taken back again. Not until it was almost beside the boat and ready for the net did we see it - the water was so opaque - but when it did show it was a sight to thrill anyone, although not such a very large fish and, I suppose, small as carp go. It weighed $8\frac{1}{2}$lb.

After that we moved to another clearing and tried again, dropping some ground-bait in the place from which the carp had just been taken. Soon I had a fish on, but lost it after two minutes, during which I had just been able to stop the run for the weeds with seventy yards of line out.

It saddened me a little to lose my first big carp and, although all lost fish must be big ones, it was a good fish. I was compensated a little ten minutes later when I landed another, but it weighed only 3lb. Then Albert caught another only a little smaller than the first.

It was time to go home to a belated breakfast; we

had proved that the impossible could be achieved and that untakeable fish can be caught, and I wondered why others had failed in the lake - was this just one day given to us by the gods? As we poled back through the weeds, preceded again by the waves of our escorts, I saw a fish leap; vertically it shot from the water, a great golden bar which fell back with a splash that set up waves that swayed the dense, matted weeds. Was it 15lb, 20lb?

I do not know, but it must have been something like that, and I began to plan our next assault when, perhaps, greater fish might fall to my rod.

But although we fished that pool for two seasons, we never caught a carp of more than 9lb, and my own best was a fish of 8½lb, taken with four others in all 34lb. We caught a lot of carp, but they seemed to average about 6lb. Furthermore, although we lost some fish, I do not think that any one of us lost or was broken by a really big carp. That the big ones did exist we knew, for we saw them leaping or rolling like pigs in the weeds, and the gamekeeper described how fish as long as his arm would persist in flocking round his boat when he was feeding the ducks with biscuits soaked in aniseed. In the end, he told us, he had to take his gun with him and shoot the fish.

I have always intended to go back to the lake and to

try floating a bait of biscuit and aniseed to the fish, but somehow I never have. We caught all our carp on honey paste and, because that was so effective, never tried worms again or parboiled potato, peas, beans, maggots, macaroni, grasshoppers, currants, raspberries and strawberries or any of the other carp baits which have been recommended from time to time by angling writers.

That may account for our failure to catch a big fellow, for small carp have a fancy for paste, and perhaps the larger fish lose the sweet tooth as they grow older. Also we never fished at night, and night is accepted by most carp fishermen as being the best time to press your suit on the monsters.

There was one very interesting thing about our fishing in that lake - this business of selection, which allows one angler to catch all the fish when he fishes with his companions in the same place, with the same sort of tackle and the same bait. He may fish with inferior skill and be possessed of less knowledge and experience, but Fate decrees that it is he who shall catch the fish. It was noticeable on several occasions with those carp, but reached its height one afternoon when my father, John Moore and I were fishing together in the boat. Now, I am one of those people who, although good at taking eels off hooks and

unmoved by most of the tricks which outrageous fortune can and does play on anglers, cannot bear
disturbance. The disturbance caused by swans, voles,
moorhens and ducks I do not mind, but when it
comes through a fellow human I find myself becoming irritated and I get all knotted up inside, because
rarely can I bring myself to be unkind or rude enough
to rebuke the person concerned. There is a relation
of mine - and I am very fond of him - who has never
learned to sit in a boat or punt without rocking it all
the while he is fishing; my wife has moments when,
in the middle of roach fishing, she will insist on put-
ting her legs over the side of the punt and paddling
her feet in the river. I remonstrate and receive the
reply, "This is as much my holiday as yours . . ." to
which, of course, there is no sensible answer. However, on this afternoon neither of them was in the
boat, and my father and John both behave quite well
in boats; but, for some reason, there was quite a lot of
disturbance, and little waves of warning and vibration
were sent out across the lake. It did not matter at all,
and I caught fish. I caught five carp, I think, and the
other two caught none. Why was it? I do not know,
for we were fishing the same place, and it was not due
to the presence of fish in any one particular place, as
there was a wind and my bait was always being

dragged a little and I caught two fish well away from the spot where the others took my bait. Our bait was the same - honey-paste made by me - and to get over the possibility of nicotine taint I, who did not smoke in those days, baited the triangles of my companions. They even fished where I had caught fish, but they did not get a bite which developed.

But, returning to our lack of success with the big fish, I have often wondered whether our method of fishing was the best. That it was successful where others had failed is true, but I cannot help thinking that today I should try out something else. Casting was the problem then, and the deep mud made ledgering impossible, but I should like to go back to that lake with a twelve-foot rod and a fixed-spool reel. The floats of leaded cork which we used must have set up some warning resistance when a fish took (and we did experience a good many abortive beginnings of bites); so I should not use those corks, but a bigger bait of honey-paste or a parboiled potato on my tri-angle, and perhaps three or four very small pieces of cork to give buoyancy to my cast from about four feet from the hook to the junction of cast and my float-ing line. I should then fish by watching the line alone and there is absolutely nothing to prevent you doing that with carp, which, once they decide to take the bait, take firmly and move off for some distance.

Also, I should ground-bait more thoroughly and more carefully, and then fish in June, July and August from dusk until breakfast-time.

After my own experiences with carp, and partly as a result of reading angling books covering a period of some 300 years, my ground-bait would consist of bread, baked hard in slices and pounded into crumbs, bran, minced whale-meat or the spleen of a cow, the guts of a rabbit chopped up, boiled potatoes and the whole mixture moistened with the water which had boiled hemp-seed and thyme (aniseed, perhaps - vide my gamekeeper). To this, if I could obtain it, I would add some of the blood of an ox and allow it to con-geal. Then, adding some live lobworms, parboiled small new potatoes, peas or beans (boiled), I would bait up the deepest hole in the lake and repeat the dose for several days until the dusk of the day I had chosen.

Arriving at the lake, I should, if possible, fish from the bank, for I do not relish sitting still in a boat for some fourteen or fifteen hours. The depth of the hole I would have ascertained; the position of my ground-bait would be marked by a cross-fix on landmarks, but, since the darkness would soon obliterate such marks and it might be necessary to make more than one cast, the amount of line required exactly to reach that spot would be measured and an imaginary line over the two forked sticks of a rod rest would point the direction. By ground-baiting over a fairly wide area I should be almost certain to cast my bait into the right place, although certainty is not a quality of night-fishing.

I would place my forked sticks in the ground so that the one nearest the water would hold the rod a little to the front of its point of balance and the second would hold the butt of the rod and the reel off the ground.

Between the sticks, and under the rested rod, there would be a ground-sheet to hold the coiled line for casting, as casting from the coil would be necessary - grass, leaves, twigs cause all sorts of complications with a coiled line, and that is to be avoided at all costs, especially when you fish blind.

Having put the baited hook in the right spot, the rod would be placed in the forks, and some three yards of line drawn off the reel and coiled loosely on the ground-sheet. In daylight the movement of the line can be seen quite clearly, but at night you need a tell-tale fixed on the loose line and illuminated by a torch. The lamp I use for that sort of fishing is equipped with a shutter so that the minimum amount of light necessary can be controlled; this light shines down on to the coiled line and tell-tale from the direction of the water, shielded from the sight of any carp which might see it. Some carp fishermen are dogmatic about the need to hide one's light from the fish, but I do not believe that a small lamp will affect the fish. Obviously you should not wave it about or flash its beam over the surface.

With the rod in position and a large landing-net ready on the left of it (it should be a really large one, if you are to net successfully a big carp in darkness; also the rim should be painted white, in order that you can see more easily when the body of the fish has been drawn in), there would be little for me to do but listen to the noises of the night as I waited for the tell-tale to twitch and the line to start moving out through the rings with gathering momentum.

If you are fresh and well-rested before the start of the operation, it is possible to sit awake throughout the dark hours, but it is well to be prepared against the cold which comes before dawn even in summer. Some people take a small tent and bedding with them, but I think that a good supply of thermos flasks and a comfortable seat is the better way, and less likely to weaken your resolve, which might lead to missing the fish of your lifetime. But, we being what we are, it is advisable to take a substitute for the visual tell-tale - a pebble which, dislodged by the movement of the line, falls into a tin. I think it is that carp addict 'BB', who tells us about a warning alarm which he and his friends use - the moving line sets a real mechanical alarm in motion and turns on a little red light.

That is an improvement upon the time-honoured pebble and tin, and no doubt there are many fishermen who can produce a similar instrument; it sounds fairly simple, but I am not much of a hand at such things, and must remain watching for the movement of a small ball of white paste, a cleft match-stick or a small piece of paper folded over the line and, when my eyes grow tired of the hypnotic strain which a tell-tale exacts, I must rely upon my pebble to bring me back to alertness.

As I said, the carp fisherman has always seemed to me to be the counterpart of the wildfowler and, indeed, they have much in common. Many are lone wolves wandering in their wilderness, or waiting, silent and alone, in the deep shadows of a tree-girt pool. I, however, prefer to enjoy my sport the more by sharing it with a companion, and because of the very nature of the places in which carp are so often found, a companion is almost an essential part of one's equipment, for, as Hugh Sheringham said, 'Night-fishing, indeed, is full of alarms, for there are noises all about, on the bank as well as on the water. It is just as well to have a good conscience if you are going to do much night-fishing.'

I have done a lot of night-fishing, and have found - as all who fish by night will discover - how difficult it is to judge the movements of a hooked fish. Your eyes are taken from you, and the feel of the rod alone is not enough - one reason for painting the rim of the landing-net white; also a very sound reason for recon- noitring the water before fishing: a day or more before. Not only should you know how the depth varies, where the weeds are and what other snags must be avoided, but you must map clearly in your mind the scene around you - the place where the bank curves in and is treacherously camouflaged by over- hanging nettles; the place where you can land your fish without danger of your rod-top first becoming caught in the branches above or your landing-net snagged on some branch or root lying below the sur- face. These may seem small things, but I recall the night when a fine sea-trout was lost because I failed to remember that a single branch reached out over the river in which I was wading: drawing the fish to the net, I felt my rod brush the branch very slightly. Slightly, but sufficiently to bend and pass under the branch and straighten a little so that the line became caught round a twig. Deprived of the play of the rod, the fish, well beaten, drifted round on a tight line. There was only one thing to do in the horror of that moment, and I jerked my rod down savagely, pulling the top free and the line away from the twig, only to find it caught over yet another and lower protrusion of that branch. The trout had waited patiently enough, but growing tired of having its head out of water protested with a feeble sideways wriggle which was quite sufficient to break the point of the cast. On another occasion a big eel came to the net in the darkness, but the net was not where I thought it was and, lifting it, I found that my cast was round the handle just below the net. That, too, was the end.

Summer is the time to catch carp, and 'BB' has told me that he believes the best month is June, as soon as the season opens. My own experience, however, has been that carp feed well in late summer as long as the weather is warm. It is warmth which matters most, and fishing is best during the night or early morning and late evening, although good fish can sometimes be taken during the heat of the day by a fisherman who can float his bait to the fish which are cruising below the surface. I say 'sometimes' because this is a method which seems to be more generally advocated by angling writers than actually employed by anglers. I have caught small carp with a surface bait, and I have seen two fair-sized fish taken on a bait fished only a few inches below, so it is worth trying, especially as at such times there is little point in trying anything else. Richard Brookes is an early writer who describes the method and suggests that at times it can be successful. 'In hot weather,' he writes, 'he (the carp) will take a lobworm at top, as a trout does a fly; or, between the weeds, in a clear place, sink it without a float, about eight inches in the water, with only one large shot on the line, which is to be lodged on the leaf of some weed. Then retire, keeping your eye upon the shot, till you see it taken away, with about a foot of the fine, and then you may venture to strike; but keep him tight, and clear of the weeds. Great numbers of carp have been taken this way.'

Brookes went on to describe the use of floating bread as bait, and that is a method suggested by many writers ever since. During the day big carp will swim just below the surface, and can be seen sampling any floating matter that interests them (I have seen them taking in mouthfuls of duck-weed); but they rarely come close to the bank unless it is to suck food from reed-stems or the under-surface of water-lily leaves. Where fishermen abound, the carp naturally tends to be shy, and swims some distance from the bank.

Your problem is to get your floating bait to the fish. Having cast your bread upon the water, you may be assisted by a breeze which will drift it out to the fish just as it takes the few hookless pieces you have scattered to attract their attention. Sometimes, however, the breeze may be so light that you must bring a sail to assist you, and it has been suggested that a lily pad attached to the cast has the advantage of acting efficiently as a sail and of seeming reasonably natural to the fish. Although I have used a drifting bait on only a very few occasions for carp, I have found it very successful with rudd, especially as the bait becomes waterlogged and begins to sink very slowly.

Unfortunately, in most lakes there are battalions of small fry which persecute your bread until it has disintegrated into small crumbs and the hook is bared; a lobworm drifting a few inches below a piece of rush, which is very buoyant, will not be attacked in this way, except where small perch swarm close to the surface, but I have never tried lobworm for carp off the bottom.

On those sultry afternoons when there is no breath in the air to help you, there is little to be done but to use a light casting reel and to assist the casting by use of a weighted float of the kind I have already described or a piece of rough stick. This should be attached to the cast as far from the hook as possible, if you intend to use a floating bait, and, after casting, you should draw it back towards you so that the bait lies on the surface at its full length from the float. Sometimes, however, even carp do surprising things, and once when fishing in this way my baited hook and the cork somehow became caught together when I cast; I was about to reel in again when I noticed the tip of a fin moving slowly through the water towards the cork, and I watched what I think was a carp of some 7 or 8lb swim slowly round the cork and then nuzzle it, its thick lips trying to suck off the bread. Had the fish been any less cautious in this attempt I might have caught it, but in the end the bread was drawn off the hook and the carp turned away with it. When I examined the cork I found that the point of the hook was sticking very lightly into the cork; whether that happened when they came together in flight or as the fish tried to draw the bread away, I shall never know, but that was the nearest I have ever been to catching a big one with a surface bait.

However, one morning, after a night's fruitless vigil beside a lake near Watford, an angler came to the swim next to mine. He was after bream, but found them no more co-operative than the carp, and following an hour's fishing without a bite he began to amuse himself with small roach, which took his maggot at every cast. He was using two maggots on a No. 16 hook, fishing them but a foot below his light quill float. Suddenly he turned to me and said, "That's queer; they were biting like mad, but I haven't had a touch for five minutes . . ." Then, as he threw a handful of maggots round his float, he added, "Probably a jack about." Musing on this, I looked at his float without any great interest just in time to see it go under and the line disappearing after it. I waited for my neighbour to tighten on the fish, and then saw that he was otherwise engaged, pouring a cup of tea from his thermos. My warning, "Look out . . .", was almost too late; he looked up to see his rod-top pulled violently down and the rod topple sideways off its rest as the reel began to revolve against the check. Unfortunately, the rod had fallen so that the handles of the reel were in the grass and could not turn with the reel. As the rod-top kicked like a living thing and was drawn round by the sideways run of the fish, my neighbour dropped his thermos and cup, scrambled for the rod, knocking his camp-stool over so that it toppled into the lake, and, clear of the grass as he lifted the butt, the reel screamed out.

On that tackle (why it held I do not know) the fight

was a long and exciting one, and I did not net his carp until some eight minutes later. But you do not want to hear too much of past battles; it is enough to say that, although his thermos was broken and he had to sit on the bank for the rest of the day, my neighbour had caught a carp weighing 6½lb.

He told me that he was glad that he had caught it, because it explained why he had been broken up quite often before when fishing in the same way.

I do not recommend surface fishing to the angler who wishes to break records. Carp like the 26lb fish taken by Mr A. Buckley from Mapperley Reservoir in 1930 are more often hooked on or close to the bed of the lake. Incidentally, Mr Buckley's fish was landed on light tackle, and was one of a bag of fish which must surely constitute a carp fisher's dream – six fish weighing 92½lb! Since then the record has been broken with a fish of 31lb 4oz from Herefordshire. But I have no right to advise you on the catching of big carp, because I have never caught one. I suppose a carp is not really considered to be big until it weighs about 16lb. So I must refer you back to the experts, and condense the thousands of words of advice which have come from their pens or have been given to me in conversation with them. Fish where there are big carp; fish at dusk, through the night and on through the day, if you can, and carry on; fish where you have put your ground-bait; fish on the bottom with lob-worm, potato or honey-paste to begin with, and try other things which come to mind when you are driven by frustration to experiment; fish quietly and fish as fine as you may when you remember the size of the fish which might take your bait. Above all, call on your British phlegm and remain calm and collected throughout all that may occur - that is, I think, asking for the impossible, but catching a really big carp is that, on the whole.

Besides the common carp there are three others to be found in Great Britain. The mirror carp, which has acquired its name through the large gleaming scales it bears along the lateral line of the body, is really an artificial fish, for it is the product of cultivation, an accident in the fish world. It grows bigger than the common carp, but it is a rarity found mainly in the south of England, where it has been established in some lakes and reservoirs. It is also known as the king carp - rightly.

Also rare is the leather carp, which is a sport of cultivation, like the mirror; it does not grow as big as the common carp, but the real dwarf of the family is the crucian, which rarely exceeds 2lb in weight, although a fish of 4lb 11oz was taken from Broadwater Lake by

Mr H. C. Hinson in 1938. It is easily distinguished from the others by the absence of barbels on the mouth and its deep body. Of course, the leather carp is so called because it lacks scales except for a few large ones generally found on the back in front of the dorsal fin or on the side of the body near the tail. The rest of the body is covered by a leathery skin.

Carp were once cultivated in stew-ponds for food, and I like to picture the monks sitting quietly by their reedy pool angling for fish which would later grace the board of the refectory. I have wondered how the monastery fared when the fish treated those fisher-men as they have on occasions treated me. Perhaps in the old days the carp fisherman possessed a finer art than we do today; certainly there were strange recipes for pastes and ground-baits, and although they bring only a smile and passing interest when we hear of them in these modern times, there may well be more to the wooing of carp than we imagine, and some day someone will study old books and emulate - as far as is legally within his power - the ancient experts.

To show him what he must be prepared to face, here are two extracts from advice given by James Chetham in 1681 when the *Angler's Vade-Mecum* was published. 'Take man's fat and cat's fat, of each half an ounce, mummy finely powdered three drams, cummin-seed finely powdered one dram, distilled oyl of annise and spike, of each six drops, civet two grains, and camphor four grains, make an ointment according to the Art.'

Perhaps, after skilful use of his weights and measures, paste and mortar, our fisherman will go out one day and beat Mr Buckley's record with his paste; perhaps he will achieve fame by treating his lobworms as the old writer suggests, 'Take the bone or skull of a dead man, at the opening of a grave, and beat the same into powder, and put of this powder into the moss wherein you keep your worms, but others like grave-earth as well'.

I shall remain content with my pure bread and honey, little potatoes, worms and, perhaps, biscuits soaked in aniseed.

Queer Fishing

H. T. Sheringham

Every species of coarse fish has, I think, given me something pleasant to remember; but the memory is not always quite what might be expected - the first memory that comes, anyhow. When I think of tench, for instance, my mind always wanders back to that long narrow pond of my boyhood, whose water was almost hidden from view by a great hedge of rhodo-dendrons, whose glowing flowers made a pageant of the scene. You had to wade through long mowing-grass to get to it. Butterflies danced about you, bees hummed drowsily in your ear, and the cooing of doves in the beech-tree at the corner of the garden invited to repose. Tench? I caught no tench. I did not even know what tench were; but I had been told that the pond contained them, and I imagined some rare exotic fishes worthy of the scene. I never expected to catch any with my useless angle; but I fished all the same, and the impressions have never been effaced.

Another pond comes before my eyes with the mention of carp, a very different pond, set in the corner of a farmyard, and filled with a sort of viscous mud which it would be erroneous to describe as water. In that queer place I angled a whole afternoon, because I was told that it contained carp. I baited with worm and paste, and sat regarding the place incredulously. Nothing happened. The float was reluctant to cock, and indeed the thinner part of the mud at the top was only four or five inches deep, so one could not expect much of it. The baits remained immovable, and after a time I got bored. Now and again there was a sort of oscillation of the liquid, which I put down to marsh gas in the act of escape, but presently I thought I saw something more tangible than that, something that seemed to wriggle near the shore. I investigated with a landing-net, and behold a veritable fish, a small carp of the oddest shape and colour, and to all appearance blind. So there were fish there after all, living the sort of amphibious life that creatures must have lived in the primeval ooze. Perhaps they were all blind like the one I caught. At any rate I did not get a bite, and, as I returned the netted fish, I did not disturb the status quo.

It was a queer fishing.

Carp

'Otter' (H. Jervis Alfred)

The carp is a beautiful fish in appearance, of a bronzy gold colour, with large scales, and having two wattles under the mouth – which is small. The fins and tail are of a dark hue, the dorsal fin extending over the greater portion of the back.

The modern names of *Cyprinus carpio* are very much alike - English, carp; French, carpe; Spanish, carpa; Italian, carpione; Swedish, karp; Danish, karpe; German, karpfe. It is a remarkably prolific fish; Bloch found 600,000 ova in a 9lb fish, and Schneider computed that there were 700,000 ova in a fish of 10lb weight; Buckland examined a fish which turned the scale at $16\frac{1}{2}$lb, its roe weighed $5\frac{1}{2}$lb and contained 2,059,750 eggs, so that the number of eggs in two such fish would equal the entire population of the metropolis. In Germany three species, known as the leather carp (so called from its having a leather-like skin, quite free from scales), the mirror carp (named from its bronzy, mirror-like appearance), and the common carp, are cultivated on such a large and profitable scale, that 'carp farming' has become quite a recognised occupation.

Carp commence spawning about May, being governed, like other fish, by the temperature; but having such an immense mass of ova to deposit, and this not being all ripe at once, it is deposited by degrees, so that the process may extend over a period of three months; the ova are deposited on weeds or flags, vivifying in about a fortnight. Their food consists of worms, insects, and the young shoots of water plants, which may possibly contribute to the somewhat muddy flavour of the fish; if caught in a lake, they will be all the better for a rest for a day or two in a box in running water before being handed to the cook.

They are a wonderfully long-lived fish, and have not unfrequently been found alive in the mud at the bottom of almost empty ponds; packed in wet moss, with an occasional reviver, in the shape of a piece of bread soaked in brandy, placed in their mouth, they may be carried in safety for almost any distance. In Holland, they are kept alive for months in cellars in damp moss, and fattened on bread and milk, having almost a cat-like vitality. What would the anti-vivisectionists of the present day say of the proceedings of Samuel Full about the middle of the last century? He cut open male and female carp, removed the milts and ovaries, and substituted for them pieces of felt, afterwards sewing together the wounds, and replacing the fish in the pond. He found that they recovered, and, growing rapidly, possessed a better flavour than fish which had not been so treated. These observations were communicated to the members of the Royal Society by Sir Hans Sloane, who was then the President.

The carp is probably the longest-lived of all our freshwater fishes, and is said in some instances to have attained the age of 200 years. Buffon tells us of carp he had seen which were known to be upwards of 150 years old. They prefer lakes and ponds to rivers; in some they grow to a large size. Salter mentions one he saw taken from the pond in Wanstead Park, facing Tilney House, which, he says, appeared much wasted from age, but weighed then 18lb; and there are fairly well authenticated records of one of 21lb taken at Bayham Abbey, near Lamberhurst, in 1870. The largest English carp was one of 24½lb taken in 1858 from the great pond at Harling, near Petersfield. In Germany they attain a still larger size; in November, 1878, the *Fishing Gazette* notice a carp weighing 40lb and three feet in length, which was caught near

Schwabach in Bavaria, and was presented to the Zoo-
logical Gardens, Frankfurt. There is also mention
made in *The Field* of February 16th, 1878, of a carp,
40 inches in length and 26 inches in girth, weighing
31lb, which was caught in the Paris district of the
Seine; but I do not remember to have seen one in
England that exceeded 16lb.

They are extremely shy fish, especially the larger
ones, which seem to increase in craftiness as they do
in weight and years. There is, however, no rule without an exception, for I have observed some splendid
fellows in the ponds of the Palace Gardens at Versailles,
which appeared to be perfectly tame, probably owing
to being fed with breadcrumbs by visitors. Until
within the last few years they have not been numerous in the Thames; though I know of a few artful old
carp which inhabit a certain deep pool at Weybridge:
they appear to glory in their extreme wisdom, and
will roll over the line, and appear to bid defiance to
the angler. Late in the month of July, 1858, on a hot
summer's afternoon, I was barbel fishing in the eddy
off Ham Point, Weybridge, the water being quite
twenty feet deep and as clear as glass. I did not so
much as touch a barbel, but took with my single rod
three magnificent carp, weighing respectively 8lb, 5lb,
and 4lb; ten eels, nine large perch, and one bream; the

carp gave quite as much play as trout. These were all taken with the lobworm, using chopped worms for ground-bait.

As a general rule the red-worm will be found the most killing bait, but they will at times prefer a well-scoured marsh-worm or lob. The majority of roach baits also are used for carp.

Use a light, stiff rod with fine running tackle and a light float, ascertaining the depth, if possible, the day before, when ground-baiting, so as to keep out of sight when you commence fishing, and disturb the water as little as you can. Throw in a few chopped worms occasionally while angling, fish on the bottom, and if in a stream strike immediately there is a bite; but if in still water or a pond, wait a second or two, till the float goes suddenly under, and then strike gently, as carp do not take the bait so quickly in dead water as in a stream, where, unless it is taken directly, it is carried away by the current and is gone.

When you have hooked a good fish use him gently and patiently; give him line, winding in and letting out, till he is exhausted. He is an exceeding strong and artful fish, and will try every possible means to get round a post or a stump, or into the weeds, so as to break the line.

The grand secret in carp fishing is to keep quiet and

fish fine. Some anglers expatiate on the great merits of boiled green peas and pieces of cherries, as very taking baits. One writer advises a worm and a gentle to be used on the hook at the same time, so as to offer the carp a choice of baits. Probably, had he suggested that a green pea and a cherry be first placed on the hook, it might have been better still; the carp could then have taken vegetables with his dinner and dessert to follow.

Fishes of the Carp Kind

Piscator (William Hughes)

Amongst all the fishes that ever put the patience of the angler to the test, the carp may fairly bear away the palm; for his extremely abstemious habits, coupled with exceeding craftiness, often prove more than a match for the skill and ingenuity of the most experienced angler. Hour after hour, and day after day, has some persevering lover of the angle planted himself by the water-side watching his tranquil float, still fishing on through heat and cold, rain, wind, calm and sunshine, not only without landing a single fish, but without even obtaining a nibble, to keep alive his hopes. But endurance like this cannot last for ever, so that at length even the value of the prize, enhanced as it doubtless is by the difficulty of obtaining it, proves insufficient to counterbalance the heavy tax that is thus laid upon the patience, and the attempt in consequence is relinquished in despair. But for all this the carp may be prevailed upon to bite, and when hooked there is no fish that shows more game, or maintains the contest for life and liberty for a longer time.

The carp is more of a pond than a river fish, although in some of the quieter parts of the latter I have found them tolerably abundant. In clay bottoms they rarely if ever take a bait freely. Walton expresses an opinion that it is more difficult to entice a carp to bite in a river than a pond; but during my practice I have experienced the exact reverse. In a small brook in Hampshire, which I had occasionally the good fortune to fish in when a boy, I seldom fished throughout the day without getting hold of a carp. My catching him was quite another matter whilst in the lower pond at Shirley near Southampton, and which was well stored with these fishes who were constantly tantalizing us by jumping some feet above water, and exhibiting their mighty dimensions; I never once got a bite from any one, though I fished in it repeatedly for several seasons, nor did I ever meet with a brother angler who in this respect had been more successful there than myself.

Before proceeding further it may not be improper to remark that there are two distinct species of fish, perfectly distinguishable from each other, both passing under the appellation of carp: a name, strictly speaking, only applicable to the larger species, the *Cyprinus carpio* of Linnaeus. The proper name of the smaller species is the gibile, or the crucian; in Warwickshire it is known by the name of crowger: and is the same fish as the *Cyprinus gebelio* of Bloch. This fish is of a much smaller size than the common carp, as it rarely arrives at the weight of two pounds; and a half a pound being the usual average; whilst the common carp has been known to exceed thirty pounds, and four or five may be considered a fair average size. Daniel, in his *Rural Sports*, notices a brace sent by a Mr Ladbroke from his park at Gatton to the then Lord Egremont, that weighed thirty-five pounds. Mr Yarrell also states that in the fishing of the large piece of water at Stourhead, where a thousand brace of killing carp were taken, the largest was thirty inches long, upwards of twenty-two broad, and weighed eighteen pounds. The same writer also mentions that there is a painting of a carp at Weston Hall, in Staffordshire, which weighed eighteen pounds and a half; and according to Jovius in lake Lurian, in Italy, carps have thriven to be more than fifty pounds weight. Bloch speaks of one that was caught near Frankfurt that was nearly nine feet long, and that weighed seventy pounds. Germany, indeed, is famed for the size of its carps, thirty or forty pounds being by no means an uncommon weight for one of these fish in many of the waters of that country: but the carps of Italy even exceed these in bulk; instances having occurred of their being taken in the lake of Como of so large a size as to weigh two hundred pounds.

The superiority in the size of the carps of Germany and Italy to those produced in our own islands, is said to be owing to the pains that are taken in those countries to select the largest fish only for breeders, whilst we, generally speaking, breed indiscriminately from all. If the matter were only properly attended to, there seems no reason why our carps should not attain as large a bulk as those of our neighbours on the continent.

But it is not the size alone that constitutes the difference between the crucian and the common carp: the former being a deeper bodied fish approaching nearer to the proportions of the roach. But notwithstanding the crucian is in every respect inferior to the common carp, it often affords the angler some amusement without much trying his patience, making up in some degree by numbers for what they are individually deficient in weight. The best bait is a moderate sized red worm without a knot, but any worm that is not too large and is well scoured will generally answer the purpose. Yet in some ponds they bite far less freely than in others; and like most other fishes they are often so capricious as to abstain from biting altogether, for several days successively, without any assignable cause. No fish indeed are so remarkably capricious in this respect as both species of the carp.

A singular instance of this occurred a few years since to two young friends of mine. They knew little of the art of angling, but hearing there was a good trout stream in the neighbourhood they bent their footsteps thither, and continued to fish away for several hours with most praiseworthy assiduity under a hot July sun, without getting even a bite, the waters having been so diminished by a long drought, as merely to trickle from pool to pool, so that no trout would venture to shew out from his hiding place. At last these two anglers chanced to light upon a deep pool, the waters of which were somewhat discoloured, either by cattle or some other cause, and here casting in their lines baited with worms of some kind or other, each of them had a bite instantly, and both succeeded in hooking a fish; which, attempting to throw out right over their heads, one broke first his rod and then his hook, whilst the other, though he saved his rod, yet it was only at the expense of losing one half his line. But as both these young gentlemen were

possessed of spare line and other tackle, the broken
rod was mended after a manner, and new lines and
hooks fitted, which were carried off one after another
in a truly wonderful manner, till at last by some accident or other one of them did manage to lug out a
carp of between four or five pounds weight. But this
was all they caught, though the fish continued to bite
away as freely as ever, till at last the whole stock of
worms was exhausted, and that amidst such a splash-
ing both in casting in and pulling out, as I suppose no
pretenders to the science of angling were ever before
or since guilty of.

The carp they did catch I saw myself on the same
evening it was taken, and well do I remember the
expression of a local shrewd and skilful angler as well
as his peculiar kind of short, dry cough, whilst he
gazed intently upon the fish and heard an account of
the boys' adventures. He looked, and coughed, and
blew his nose, then looked and coughed again.

An early hour on the following day found him by
the side of this self same pool, the whereabouts of
which he had contrived to elicit from the two young
anglers, and which if he had entertained any doubt
about, the footmarks around the brink, and disturbed
state of the loose gravel, coupled with the circumstance of his finding a silk handkerchief belonging to

one of the parties, would have proved the identity of the spot, yet not a bite could this most cunning angler obtain there throughout the day, the whole of which he spent by the side of this self-same pool, buoyed up with the constant hope that within a minute or two the sport would begin. The carp could not have moved out of this pool in the interim, as from the extreme lowness of the waters all communication was cut off from the neighbouring pools. A willow bush that grew partly in the water precluded anyone from effectually netting the place.

During the winter months carps bury themselves in the mud or weeds, where it is probable they remain embedded in a state of torpor and without food during the whole of that period. In that truly interesting work, White's *Natural History of Selborne*, it is stated, that 'In the gardens of the Black Bear, in the town of Reading, is a stream, or canal running under the stables, and out into the fields on the other side of the road; in this water are many carps which lie rolling about in sight, being fed by travellers who amuse themselves by tossing them bread; but as soon as the weather grows at all severe, these fishes are no longer seen, because they retire under the stables, where they remain till the return of spring.'

Certain it is that carps rarely take a bait till the warm

weather has set in; though Walton observes, some have been so curious as to say the 10th of April is a fatal day for carps; but this I am inclined to think is far too early in the season, unless the spring be an unusually mild one, though if there is any truth in the assertion we so often hear made by old people that the seasons are much later than they used to be, the elapse of a couple of centuries which has taken place since honest Izaak's time, may have effected this difference.

Aristotle and Pliny say that the carp spawns six times in a year; but in this country it seems that it occurs but once during that period, and takes place about the months of May and June, some spawning earlier, and others later, as is the case with the salmon and many other fishes. At the time of spawning the female is usually attended by two or three males, and the ova being cast on the flags and weeds is there impregnated by the males, and in the course of about ten days it is enlivened.

In waters that agree with them, carps usually attain the weight of three pounds at about their sixth year, which doubles by about the time they reach their tenth year, that being, according to Sir Francis Bacon, the limit of their existence, though Dubravius extends this period to thirty years, whilst more modern authorities contend that he lives for upwards of a century, and sometimes attains to even double that age. When the infirmities of old age begin to creep upon them, their scales assume a greyish cast, which as they grow older become still paler, and at these times they are subject to a disease that often terminates fatally, the head and back becoming overspread with a moss like excescence; (a disorder indeed with which young carps are sometimes affected,) as also to eruptions under the scales. They also suffer occasionally from intestinal worms. But to whatever age a carp may live in his own element, it seems perfectly clear that no kind of fish whatever will live so long out of it.

In Holland it is a very common practice not only to keep them alive out of their proper element for a month or more, but even to fatten them, by inclosing them in wet moss suspended in a net, and feeding them with bread and milk, taking especial care to refresh them from time to time by throwing water over the moss. In winter they are transported alive to a considerable distance packed in moistened moss, linen, or snow, with a piece of bread steeped in brandy in their mouths, to keep up their spirits during the journey.

In our own country it is a very common practice to keep carp in a clear run of water before they are killed for the table, in order to get rid of the rank flavour they are apt to imbibe from the weeds and muddy bottom of the waters they usually inhabit.

The merits of the carp as an article of food, are too well known to require any comment, and well stewed either in port wine or claret, can be equalled by few, and exceeded by none. Caviar is sometimes made of the roe of the female fish, which is considered equal to that of the sturgeon, and is in high repute amongst the Jews, as the sturgeon being a fish without scales is unclean by their law, and therefore an abomination to all true Israelites. Carps may also be improved in their edible qualities by being deprived of their generative organs; a discovery first made by one Samuel Fuller, who opening the ovary of the carps, and taking out the eggs from the females, and the milts from the males, made up for their deficiency with a piece of old hat, taking especial care at the same time not to injure either the urethra or rectum, and uniting the wound by a suture.

And now for the baits wherewith to inveigle this crafty fish. The bait I have ever found the most successful is a well scoured red worm of moderate size, or a couple of brandlings baited as before directed for catching trout. I have tried pastes of various kinds, but have rarely succeeded well with any of them; though I have known persons who when fishing with paste for roach have unexpectedly hooked a lusty carp; and many there are who give a decided preference to paste in carp fishing to any other kind of bait whatever.

The following is a good receipt for making paste Take the flesh of a rabbit cut small and some flour (bean flour is the best). Mix these together with a little honey, and pound them in a mortar; white wool may also be mixed up with it to cause it to adhere the more toughly together. Another sort of paste is also recommended, made of bean's flour, rabbit's fur, bees wax, and mutton suet, beat up together in a mortar, with a little clarified honey tempered before the fire, and stained with vermilion.

Baiting the ground you intend to fish over a day or two previously, and keeping it constantly baited in the interval will greatly enhance your chance of success. Grains and bullock's blood, mixed with cow dung and grains, are considered to make an excellent ground bait; as do also grains mixed with greaves. Some pellets of the kind of paste you intend to angle with should also be thrown in upon the ground bait, in order to enable the carp duly to appreciate their edible qualities. Carps will also bite at gentles, cadis, and most kind of grubs; they will often bite at a whitish coloured grub that is usually found under cowdung, but as these are very tender, a bristle should be tied to the arming wire of the hook, which standing out upward will keep the bait from sliding down, and so presenting an untempting appearance. A carp, it is also said, will take green peas, and cherries, with the stones taken out, currants, gooseberries, and other fruit, none of which I have ever tried; but from the partiality of the carp to a vegetable diet, it is very probable some of these might prove successful, as it is well known they are extremely fond of lettuce leaves; whilst Bloch assures us that the leaves and seeds of salad particularly agree with them, and that they fatten upon them more speedily than upon any other kind of food whatever.

From the extreme wariness of the carp, every angler who wishes to catch him must be careful at all times to keep well back from the water's edge, and never to take a stand on high ground. The most certain plan is to lay down the rod, and standing back watch it from a short distance. Few indeed are aware of the number of fishes they scare away from their baits by standing close to the water-side and holding their rods in their hands; for although the water may be too foul to enable the angler to see the fishes, they may nevertheless be able to see the angler. Carp too, when roving about in foraging parties, keep moving up and down, often rising to the very surface to look around them, as well as to seize upon some of the gnats that are playing about there, when, if they detect any object that excites their fears, off they dart, and do not probably return again to the same spot for the rest of the day. No fish that inhabits the fresh water is so suspicious as the carp, so much so indeed that it is rarely they can be prevailed to approach sufficiently near a boat to be angled for from it with any chance of success, though the wary trout does not seem to have any such fears; in fact more of the latter fish are commonly taken from a boat in lake fishing, than by angling from the shore.

Also consider that in angling for carp, many valuable chances have been thrown away by adopting a prettily painted float, which, when standing proudly erect in the water, attached to a line set off with three or four round leaden pellets within a few inches of the bait, which hangs suspended about midwater, presents altogether a truly traplike appearance. The instinct in most animals that enables them to detect a trap is truly wonderful, and some degree of ingenuity is absolutely necessary to empower you to outwit so subtle a fish as a carp. As for myself I have ever found it the most successful plan whenever I have used a worm, always to let the bait rest on the bottom, and either to use no float at all, or a small piece of common cork with a mere slit in it to fix it to the line, and this I invariably keep at least a yard or two from the bait. By adopting this mode, the gut to which the hook is fastened, as well as the whole line affair, is more likely to escape the attention of the fishes, who are not so likely to notice it, when lying quietly along the ground, as if hanging suspended from the float in the water, consequently they then seize upon the bait with less hesitation; which, having once tasted the sweets of, they will not afterwards so readily abandon. Nor is there any great difficulty in detecting a bite when fishing in this manner, for the slightest agitation of the line will be communicated to the float, which as the fish moves off, as a carp almost invariably does, will be put either in active motion, or disappear at once under water. As soon therefore as the slightest movement is discovered, advance quick but cautiously, and seizing hold of the rod raise it gently till you get all the stray line out of the water, reeling up some portion of it if the fish shapes his course towards you, and getting the line nearly tight, 'then fix with gentle twitch the barbed hook', which you may rest assured the fish no sooner feels, than he will at once make a desperate rush off, and then probably leap to some considerable distance out of water. The effects of the first rush of the carp is what you must be particularly prepared for, as his progress is often so rapid as to cause a dead strain on the line before the rod can be sufficiently elevated to bring it into proper play, and if a carp of any size succeeds in doing this, your hook or line are sure to give way. He will also not unfrequently contrive, after leaping out of water to fall back upon the line in such a manner as to snap it right off. At such a time the line should be suddenly slackened; for being a leather-mouthed fish there is no danger of his getting unhooked, as there would be in the instance of a trout or a salmon under such circumstances.

It also sometimes occurs, that in spite of all you can do to prevent it, but prevent it you must if possible, that a carp will run in amongst the weeds; in doing this he very often gets you fouled and breaks the tackle; but instead of this it often occurs that he detaches some portion of the weeds which adhere to the line, in which case let him lug about his burden to his heart's content, and never attempt to relieve him of it, as by this means it is probable he will tire himself out much quicker than you could effect by any contrivance of your own; and above all things, don't attempt to land him till he is thoroughly beaten, otherwise the event is not very likely to occur at all.

Although carps are very fond of sporting about on the surface, frequently leaping several feet out of water, yet they are rarely taken either with a natural or artificial fly, though sometimes a grasshopper sunk beneath the surface proves an attractive bait. The best time for fishing for carp is just before sunrise in the morning, and during the twilight of an evening. More may be done in half an hour at those times, than during an entire summer's day, as both early and late they approach the shore in search of food. The best places to angle in at such times, are in the clear shallow edges of the pond, particularly outside rushes if any should chance to grow there, or upon a gravel bottom, if there is any such in the pond; particularly such spots as cattle are in the habit of frequenting. In the day time, open spaces between the weeds are the most likely spots, though it is exceedingly difficult to get a weighty fish out of such places when you have succeeded in hooking him.

Carp from a Puddle near the Sea

David Marlborough

Some years ago I was on holiday in a small town on the East Coast. As I did not fancy sea fishing from the beaches, I went to the local 'tackle shop' to ask about the freshwater fishing prospects. It was really a general hardware store, but the dealer seemed a quite keen angler, and he was able to tell me that the only freshwater fishing locally was 'the pond down by the railway'. I left the shop hoping that I'd stumbled on some undiscovered Redmire - but I was to be quickly disillusioned.

It was in a scruffy field, behind some houses, on the outskirts of town. A funnel-shaped depression lay in the middle of the pasture, and in that lay what at first sight appeared to be nothing more than a puddle. No vegetation grew round its banks, and there was none in the water. which was the colour of tea. I don't suppose you could have put a cricket pitch into it without leaving the stumps at either end on dry land. The only things in its favour were the depth and its reputation as the only carp pond for miles around.

That evening saw me on its banks, a light roach rod, 3lb line and a crust of bread in my hand. I soon discovered why the locals found carp fishing so difficult! Few people tried the pond, only pensioners and small boys, and they were uniformly armed with storm lanterns, beach-casting rods, and float tackle set 18 inches deep on massive cuttyhunk lines, and tied direct to the tip-rings, roach-pole fashion.

Every evening that week, I had the pond virtually to myself. I would fish intently until about midnight, then pack up, by which time there would be a wild carp of 2 - 3lb in the net, and occasionally two. Small fish, you might say - but what good fighters on light tackle, and how surprising to get them at all from such a tiny water!

The only snag was that it was so near the coast, and cold sea-breezes kept the temperature oscillating about 60⁰F. If the water temperature was below 60 degrees. I caught wild carp on ledgered paste; if it went above, I caught them on floating crust and the occasions I caught a brace were the warmest nights. Undoubtedly I would have got more if the weather had been warmer, but I was well satisfied. Apparently my successes were considerably more frequent than the locals', but this was no measure of anything except appropriate tackle.

This might seem a trifling example, but in fact, I learnt two important lessons from fishing this pond. Firstly, I confirmed the importance of 60^0 for top or bottom feeding in ponds; secondly, I found fishing such a tiny water was well worth while for the sheer enjoyment of catching those game little 'wildies'.

I live in an area in which many clubs do not own waters of their own. They exist solely to get enough people together to hire a weekly coach. They will cheerfully travel miles every weekend to fish in large, well-known waters - only to return in the evening practically fishless. This is a pattern which is repeated week after week throughout the season. They may not even visit the same water twice. In other words. they get wide experience, but not really intimate knowledge of any of the waters they fish This is just not the pattern for achieving consistent results. I know many extremely good anglers, and they all started by fishing waters near at hand. They got to know them in all their moods, and regarded an occasional outing as a treat.

It's not as if the 'coach-anglers' have no water close at hand. This may be true of the industrial North, but

certainly not of the London green belt, which is dotted with small ponds and streams, relics of vanished
farms and great houses. Too many of these anglers
ignore such waters; true, many are no bigger than the
'puddle' I have described, but for all that, fishing them
is great fun, and even a 2lb carp is a more pleasant
adversary - and larger - than the average fish their far-
ranging outings seem to provide.

There is an object lesson for us all in that puddle. If
we search them out, and accept their standards, we
can get a great deal of enjoyment from the smallest
and most unlikely of local waters And they are splendid places for the beginner to learn.

When the Carp Fed like Roach

Peter Tombleson

There are few occasions when fish feed completely out of character, and of all the species the carp is the one least likely to do so. That's my experience, or at least, it was until last summer. It was then that I fished a lake in which the carp fishing could only be described as out of this world. Mind you, I had to go to Czechoslovakia to find it.

So far, very few British anglers have had the opportunity to fish behind the Iron Curtain, but Bill Taylor, of Oxford, and I were lucky enough to spend a week in Czechoslovakia last year. We were invited to fish and comment on the fishing, primarily because this eastern European state wants to encourage visitors.

Czechoslovakia is a small country that was once the hunting domain of the royal houses of Europe. It is dotted with lakes and criss-crossed with streams and rivers, all holding most of the species of fish we know, as well as some others. But if one species is to be found in large numbers it is the carp.

In England we tend to regard the carp rather as Indians regard a totem pole - as an emblem of prestige, with reverence almost. This is because fishing for big carp is a difficult sport and one that calls for dedication. But on the Continent the carp is not so highly regarded sportingwise. Its prestige arises from its culinary attraction, for the carp is a delicacy, more so as one moves east across Europe. It is served up at Christmas time with the ceremony that we reserve for turkey, for goose. Carp have been bred in Europe for many years to provide food and sport, and in Czechoslovakia, where they also breed pike and pike-perch they know a great deal about these fish.

Bill Taylor and I fished only on two occasions for carp, but both times we had astonishing sport. The water was a small lake at Trebon in southern Bohemia. The lake bed was hard and gravelley, not a bit like the muddy-bottomed lakes in which carp grow so well in this country. We chose our swims and I swam into mine to pull up clumps of reed growing out from the side. During the day the sun was so hot that it was more comfortable to be in the water than out, for apart from a few small roach and perch, nothing was caught until the sun dipped behind the skyline.

It was then almost as if someone had turned on a switch, priming the fish to bite. We were both fishing with Czechoslovakian dumpling, which is one of the main items of the local diet. It is very similar to Norfolk dumpling but perhaps not so light and is served in every café and hotel, and one can either eat it or buy it as fish bait - a very handy arrangement!

My first cast with a knob of this dumpling paste on a No. 8 hook had been completed only a few seconds before the float slid away and I connected with a miniature torpedo. After threshing the water for several minutes at the expense of my rod top a carp of about 3lb came sulkily to the net. I decided to change my rod to a built-cane P.T. float-rod and use a stronger line.

From then on until darkness I caught a carp at practically every cast. They took the bait either off the bottom or on the bottom, and invariably fought like little demons. But despite this, other fish came into the swim. And a few yards away Bill Taylor was also hammering out the carp just as fast as he could go.

Out in the main lake we could hear great splashes as big fish turned over, but in vain we tried to catch larger fish. Four pounds was the best we could manage. Bill caught a tench and I caught a common bream as well as a few rudd and roach.

All the others were common carp, fully scaled, and most appeared to be of the same year group. It seems that they tended to rove the sides of the lake at dusk and dawn feeding ravenously and taking bait like feeding roach. It was useless to fish during the heat of the day. From dawn until sunrise the next day we caught fish but then it was all over and we had to move on and resume our journey back to Prague.

Our guide and interpreter, Emmanuel Kutera, took the bream and tench for eating when we returned our carp to the water. In the space of a few hours we had caught over 30 carp, all on light tackle and all from the edge of a lake the potential of which we could only guess at. This sort of fishing is common enough in Czechoslovakia and we were sorry that we could not spend more time exploring the smaller lakes which abound with tench, carp and bream.

It is some comfort to know that the Czechs, realising the potential of their fishing, which also offers trout, catfish and pike-perch, are planning to open the country to visiting anglers from the West.

I hope that those who follow in our footsteps will find the carp feeding as we did

The Fish with a Sixth Sense

Dick Kefford

From time to time we read or hear of instances when thought-transference between man and animals appears, on the available evidence, to be manifest. I have read of big-game trackers who would warn the man with the gun on the approach of the quarry 'not to think of them' or the game would sense his presence - a belief widespread in all countries among those who live close to nature.

It has been said that a sixth sense tells some carp anglers when a carp, unseen and unheard, is approaching their baited hooks. I cannot truthfully say that this has happened to me, but there have been occasions when, for a number of possible reasons, I have fished with greater confidence, almost with a feeling of near-certainty of a carp run - and sometimes it has happened, too!

My experience, however, shows that the quarry is

more receptive to this supposed impulse than the angler. I have been interested in carp and carp angling for about 15 years, and I must have spent almost as much time observing the fish as in fishing for them, so fascinating do I find them.

I remember on one occasion creeping about in the dense osier bed at Redmire and watching an enormous mirror carp in a sheltered bay. This giant was busy routing in the lake bed and was shielded from sight of me by a cloud of billowing mud. Every now and again a shovel-sized tail broke surface as the great fish foraged in the shallow water. Although I remained perfectly still, that carp seemed to sense that all was not well and, leaving its feeding, glided unhurriedly, but purposefully, to mid-lake.

In the early years at Redmire we ground-baited and fished at the dam end. After a fish or two had been hooked and lost we discovered that if we stayed on the bank all night, though keeping well back from the water's edge and hardly moving, the coming of daylight would reveal our ground-bait undisturbed on the bottom; yet if we spent the night in the tent every scrap of ground-bait would have been cleaned up - and not by the ducks either!

More recently at Redmire, John Nixon caught a 23lb fish of which he afterwards wrote: 'I sat watching the by-now familiar quartet of carp around my bait. It is difficult to watch a bait for long periods and I suppose *my attention must have wandered,* for when I looked back the bait had gone. That in itself was not startling. Many times before, the bait had seemingly 'disappeared', temporarily obscured by one of the carp, and my gaze dropped to the rod-tip to check that the line was still slack. But it wasn't. It was moving up and away in a rapidly tightening arc, and with a wildly thumping heart I picked up the rod and struck.' The italics are mine, for those words, in my opinion, are the vital ones.

This year I was at Redmire in early August for a weekend's fishing with my brother and 'BB'. Only one carp became interested in our carefully presented baits. 'BB' had spent a long time fishing a swim at the dam end of the lake where earlier he had glimpsed two large carp. Eventually he decided to see how I had fared at a swim on the shallows. Perhaps 10 minutes had passed when across the breadth of the lake came the rasping noise of 'BB's reel ratchet. Not unexpectedly, on his hasty return 'BB' found the line extending out into a weed-bed and the carp departed - but I wonder whether a run would have occurred had he stayed, waiting, by his rod?

Another night I recall was in July, some years ago, when I was fishing as a guest at a lake in Sussex. We were divided into small groups fishing the few available pitches around the lake. A late-comer, tired after a week's work and long journey from London, settled down to fish in one of the remaining pitches, and soon, having put up his tackle, cast and set his bite-alarm, he was asleep.

About midnight a steady and prolonged alarm from his buzzer was heard by everyone around the lake except himself, and then after an interval of silence came the sleepy cry: "My spool's half-empty!" Many baits were out that night, but it had to be the neglected one which brought the only carp run.

How often, after long hours of fruitless watching and waiting by the rod, anglers have temporarily left their tackle and then had a run develop, I hesitate to think. In the early days I used to put it down to the cussedness of fate, but it happened so often that I began to think seriously about other more realistic causes. It was then that I began to believe that there is something in this telepathy.

I don't know what others think about when they are fishing, but when I began carping I had the 'bug' so badly that as soon as I started fishing I found myself mentally contemplating the hidden leviathans and subconsciously exerting will-power in an effort to get the fish on the hook, if not on the bank! If there is any fact in the theory of telepathy, it is not surprising that it was four hard-fished seasons before I caught a size-able carp!

I have since taken a number of carp in the 10-20lb range, but never yet one of greater weight. Perhaps this will come eventually if I see that the reel line is reasonably strong and I think about anything other than catching carp. I may even accept the recommendation of that former doyen of carp angling, Otto Overbeck, who recommended the carp angler to read, 'a book of a kind to aid the mind in being peaceful and patient'.

Carp in South Africa

J. H. Yates

Some time ago, I received a letter from Mr Richard Walker, holder of the British record for carp. His attention had been drawn to one of my weekly articles in the Johannesburg *Sunday Times*, in which his claim to the Empire Record was disputed. He stated, among other things, that he had not known of the 44lb 12oz mirror-carp caught by Mr Smithers in Florida Lake in 1946; and subsequent correspondence has led me to believe that a little light on carp and carp-anglers in the Union of South Africa might be of interest to readers of *Angling*.

I understand, for instance, that the Carp Catchers' Club is an exclusive body that admits no new members until they have caught a carp weighing at least 10lb. Believe me, if the same conditions were applicable in South Africa, the Club's membership would run into thousands. What is more, their ages would vary from six to seventy-six. I have a letter before me as I write, in which a proud mother says:

Brakpan, 11.5.53
Once again I would like to tell you about my small son aged nine. He beat his Dad and all competitors at the Van Dyke Angling Outing by landing a carp weighing 14^1/$_2$ lb. His Dad's carp weighed 13^3/$_4$ lb.

It might also be mentioned that were the entrance qualification raised to the capture of a 20lb carp, there would still be hundreds of eligibles. As a matter of fact a 20lb carp excites but little attention here. They are too common.

Let me give you a little of the history of the carp in this country. They were introduced into the Cape Colony in 1897. The idea, at the time, was that they should be put into farm dams and so provide the farmers with both a welcome change of diet and a little sport. These fish, finding conditions very much to their liking, grew quickly and bred in an incredible manner. It became the fashion to have a carp-dam and they spread slowly northwards to the Orange Free State and the Transvaal. The Homestead Dam, Benoni – one of a string of dams in that area – was the first to be stocked in 1904. There they multiplied so prolifically that thousands of fingerlings were taken to other dams all over the Transvaal and even as far as the northern Cape.

As time went on, however, it became obvious that carp in either a farm, irrigation or town dam were far from being an asset. They fouled the water to such an extent that, in many cases, cattle refused to drink. It was also found that the water was of little use for irrigation purposes; and in some cases the purity of a town's water supply was threatened, as in the case of Bethlehem in the Free State.

There the water became so contaminated that purification costs rose to staggering figures; and in desperation and because they had no suitable equipment of their own, the Town Council was driven finally to hire the services of Durban's deep-sea fishermen. For days the dam was dragged with huge nets, and tons of carp ranging from 3 to 35lb in weight were dumped into waiting railway trucks and taken away to be buried. The waters were then heavily stocked with black bass. This was a costly business but the water was saved. In the meantime Provincial Councils began to take notice and legislation was enacted which made it an offence to transfer carp from one dam to another. But the laws of man had no control over Nature. Year after year heavy rains, cloudbursts and floods swept the contents of farm dams into the nearest river; and in their new unrestricted quarters the carp bred and spread like a plague.

Today there is scarcely a river in the Transvaal, and there are certainly none in the Free State, which is not thick with carp. Natal is not badly affected as yet, but many fear that it is only a question of time. So there you have the position, we have hundreds of dams and thousands of miles of river simply teeming with carp.

From the point of view of carp anglers, and they can be numbered in their thousands, the position is very satisfactory. The major attraction is, of course, the fact that you never know when you are going to hook a really big one. A big one out here means a fish weighing 25lb or more.

I should not like to give the impression that carp fishing in South Africa is just a matter of making a cast and hauling in a fish, far from it. Our carp are just as capricious and as tantalizing as those in any other part of the world. We have carp-dams in the centre of Johannesburg and for thirty miles to the east and West, where every weekend each one has its quota of patient carp anglers. Little or no ground-baiting is done and the anglers, who usually use two rods, bait their hooks, cast as far as they can, then sit down to wait. Sometimes they wait weeks.

The most popular bait is mealie-meal with a touch of flour, cooked until it is just stiff enough to stay on the hook; and flavourings are often used of which curry powder is a great favourite.

Occasionally the carp forsake the usual bait and take an unusual lure. For instance, in the Kleinfontein dam (one of the Benoni string), carp have been taken on the artificial fly by Freddie Vogt, a keen bass angler, who, as Kleinfontein is well stocked with large-mouths, was trying to tempt one of them with a Cardinal. He got a heavy pull and for a time thought he was playing a record bass. It turned out to be a $5\frac{1}{2}$lb. carp. He was inclined to regard his catch as a fluke but had to change his mind when, a little later, he caught two more on the same fly.

A recent and most interesting catch was made by Mr Campher of Brakpan. He was fishing in the Vaal river near Parys when his bait - mealie-meal - was taken by a strong fish which took him thirty-five minutes to land. It was a 25lb scale carp in excellent condition. Subsequent examination showed the fish was totally blind; in fact, it had neither eyes nor eye-sockets. How a blind fish could survive in a river like the Vaal, which teems with predacious yellow-fish and catfish to say nothing of otters, cormorants and water tortoise, is a mystery.

In conclusion I might say that while the present South African record stands at 44lb 12oz, it will not, in my view, be long before it is broken. Carp estimated to weigh as much as 60lb *have often been seen*; and there is one giant in Florida Lake which, if it is ever brought to land, will astonish the world.

A Carp from Mapperley Shallows

John Norman

Writing in Angling *in 1953, Richard Walker said that the outstanding individual carp-fishing feat of 1952 was John Norman's capture at Mapperley of an 18¹/₂ lb fish. This account, taken from Mr Norman's first-hand story, provides a clear insight into the lengths to which carp fishing enthusiasts went in pursuit of these elusive fish, by way of both carefully planned tactics and personal discomfort.*

Quite recently a great contemporary angler wrote: 'Never do anything (when fishing) without knowing why you are doing it.' Had I heeded his advice I might have been successful at Mapperley lake much sooner than was actually the case; and, in the hope that others may profit by them, I write this account of my exploits there.

In 1930, the late Albert Buckley caught four carp at Mapperley, the smallest of which weighed 9lb and the largest, a 26-pounder, created a record. All these fish were taken between the hours of 9am and 1pm and both the circumstances of these captures and particulars of the tackle which he used were widely publicized.

When, in 1951, I had my first opportunity to fish this lake, Buckley's ways and means were deeply impressed upon my mind and every word which he had written about this memorable occasion I had studied carefully.

The result of my inquiries among the regulars at the lake were rather disheartening. It appeared that in 1930 Buckley had caught the four fish to which I have referred and two others which weighed respectively 14 and 16lb. Then between 1930 and 1947 he caught only two fish, one which weighed 19½lb in 1932, and a 13-pounder in 1947; and during the same period his two friends, Messrs A. Innocent and L. Brown, took three carp between them from the lake.

Here was a poser. Why had this water yielded only five carp in seventeen years?

I may have been presumptuous, but I had my doubts when I found Buckley writing:

'The carp can only be caught when strong winds drive them from their natural haunts, the weedy shallows, to the deep water at the embankment end.'

This seemed to me to supply a possible reason for the fact that he and his friends had caught few fish with considerable intervals between each capture. The windy conditions which they favoured were abnormal and occurred infrequently. Should these, however, prevail when they were fishing for carp, they sometimes caught one; and I am told (by locals) that Mr Buckley and his friends only fished for these carp in deep water.

But I was not satisfied that Buckley was right in his contention that it was impossible to fish the Mapperley Shallows successfully; and determined to make the attempt.

Buckley used a roach rod, 4x gut and a fine line being convinced that only gossamer tackle could deceive big carp. Clearly 4x gut was useless where snags abounded and I decided to use a stouter rod and a 6lb b.s. monofilament line, which was subsequently replaced by one of 9lb b.s. It was at about this time that I made contact with 'BB' and Walker who both approved my choice. Walker held that:

'As long as at least six feet of line lie on the bottom its thickness, within reason, does not matter.'

This he reinforced by stating that he had caught large carp using a 12lb b.s. line *tied direct to the hook*. He was, however, satisfied that carp are always suspicious of even the finest tackle, if it rises vertically anywhere near the bait. My home-made rod, which he generously helped me to make to his design, is a powerful two-piece split-cane, but it is light and supple enough to flick a ball of paste on an unleaded line, thirty yards with ease. A large fixed-spool-reel and a capacious landing-net completed the gear.

Having got my tackle into what I am sure was shipshape, I received still further guidance from my two mentors. 'Carp,' they said 'feed in the shallows and among weeds under normal summer conditions. They seldom frequent deep water, which is comparatively sterile, especially at depths of more than 20 feet or so, to which they repair only when the shallows are cold.' Here they were in agreement with Buckley. From this it appeared that armed with the correct tackle and knowledge of the normal haunts of the fish, I had only to fish carefully and a Mapperley carp would soon be mine. There was, however, an early snag. Mapperley Lake is 29 acres in extent, and is in the main shallow, including some parts which are far out in the lake. Many of the marginal shallows are moreover inaccessible during the early months of the season because the water runs up among the willows on its fringe.

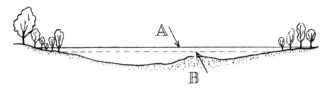

Mapperley Lake. Winter to June water level is shown at A. B shows August level.

Mapperley Lake supplies water to several collieries and its level falls four feet in an average summer between June and August.

If I were to succeed, it seemed imperative to cut an open fishing space among the saplings close to a promising piece of water. This I did, and heart-breaking work it was, which apart from one abortive run produced no success.

Although I saw carp cruising in the shallows where I fished they were not feeding there; and it was not until late in the year that I found out why.

Carp like a bolt-hole, and they feed more freely in the shallows when there is deep water nearby; it was tedious work finding such a place with plummet and float. But I searched the bed of the lake on many occasions until I found what appeared to be the ideal spot, namely a two-foot shallow which sloped away to six feet of water on either side of an extensive but thin weed-bed where, I reasoned, both food and shelter were available to the fish.

I baited up this swim carefully and although the place was too difficult to fish at the time since it was necessary to wear gum boots to bait it, I resolved to fish it when the water level fell. Burglars intervened, however. Three of my neighbours were robbed and clearly I could not go off on night fishing expeditions until my wife's peace of mind was restored, by which time that particular carp season was over.

Then in 1952 my faith in this carefully sought venue was justified, despite some qualms on account of a number of hazards. On my right was the weed-bed thirty yards wide but not too thick; in front of me lay an open lane of water which stretched right out into the lake; but danger threatened to the left front where fallen willows littered the shallows and large trees stretched out their snake-like roots into the water. It looked very promising nevertheless and I cast out a large ball of paste on my hook and surrounded it with many similar ones. Then I threw in a honey 'bomb'. These 'bombs' contain liquid honey in a cardboard carton which is sealed with a thick cellophane top. This cellophane disintegrates in time and the honey oozes out slowly. With my rod on its rest I hid myself and listened all night to huge carp as they splashed and wallowed near by.

Then at 5.15am I had a run! The line whipped through the rings, I left my cover, flicked over the pick-up of my reel and tightened. Eighty yards away the fish circled then tore towards a

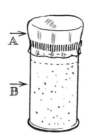

Honey Bomb

A: Cellphane cap

B: Carton containing liquid honey.

tangle of dead willows to my left. Floundering through a shallow bay to my right, I wound in furiously to take in a great belly in the line. Happily, by the time the carp came near to the snags I was able to recover all the slack. It bored heavily and I'm sure I tipped that fish head over heels so to speak when I put on the final pressure which turned it with only inches to spare. From then on the fish kept to the open water in front and except for a last-minute fumble when I tried to net it with trembling hands, there was little cause for worry. As the needle of my steel-yard wobbled between $18^1/_2$ and 19lb, my feelings were mixed. True, it was the first carp to be taken from the Mapperley Shallows, but was it mine? Only one pair of hands had handled the rod but more than one brain had helped to accomplish the downfall of this fish.

It must not be the last; and, if my experience of

tackling a difficult and extensive water is of help to others, it is a pleasure to pass it on.

Christmas Carp
J. K. Ebblewhite

Whilst appreciating the danger of contradicting experts, I will relate two angling experiences which appear to constitute decided exceptions to the following statements made by two eminent biologists.

'In winter carp cease feeding, withdraw to deep holes and bury themselves in the mud, Where they remain in a torpid state till the spring.' (A. F. Magri MacMahon in *Fishlore*)

'The minimum temperature for feeding is also a critical limit for growth, for in fasting periods fish lose weight . . . for carp this limit is 59 degrees . . .' (H. Chapman Pincher, *Angling* No. 40, The Effects of Temperature Change on Fish.)

Until quite recently some of my 'in-laws' lived near a lake in Cheshire which contains very large carp, as the result of which my visits combined duty with pleasure. The lake is about a mile long, some thirty yards wide and has an average depth of about two feet. One side is open to lawns and parkland whilst the other is shaded by tall trees and overhung by straggling rhododendron bushes. It is part of a once lovely pleasure ground, but heavy taxation has left its mark in promiscuous growth and decay. The lake is nowhere more than four feet deep and a large area does not exceed a foot in depth. During the summer the water is almost entirely blocked with what I take to be water milfoil which sinks below the surface during the winter months.

Early last November (1946), when carp have supposedly retired to their winter quarters, I was in Cheshire for the weekend. On the morning of the second I strolled down to inspect my 'hole' and found a 'local' fishing there in a very desultory manner. It was a cold, damp day and nothing was moving. The angler said that it was unusual for him to come out so late in the season but he had fancied an hour with the small roach which are the only other inhabitants of the water. After lunch the sun came out, dispelling the cold mist, so I hied me to the 'hole', cast in my gear and settled down to a quiet smoke.

To my amazement I had several nibbles which were

undoubtedly the handiwork of a carp. I tried again on the following Monday, November 4th, and had quite an exciting day, losing several and grassing two carp weighing a little over two pounds and slightly over three pounds respectively. There may be nothing extraordinary about this, though I have never known carp to move so late in the season and during a cold spell, but my next experience really did shake me!

December 24th, 1946, found me once more in Cheshire after a miserable drive through freezing fog. On Christmas Day a stroll round the lake showed it to be covered with ice. By the twenty-seventh my 'hole' was clear though considerable patches of ice remained nearby. At about 10am on the morning of the twenty-eighth as I passed along the lake, patches of thin ice were noticeable here and there. But when my 'hole' was reached I had the shock of my life. It was full of carp - one layer over another plainly visible in the shallow sunlit water. I had never seen such a concentration of fish even in high summer.

It was approaching 12.30pm when I reached the house to find that packing operations had not commenced, so seizing my tackle I was soon eagerly watching my float in the 'hole'. The sun was now off the water and no fish were visible but my float sank slowly, I struck gently and out came a half-pound roach. (It is my practice to tighten very gently on a carp till the hook finds lodgement. It is then usually possible to lead the mystified fish round and round the confined limits of the pool and by the time it becomes frightened it is too tired to make a meteoric dash into the weeds and safety.) I rebaited and cast again.

Almost immediately the float showed those symptoms which denote a suspicious carp attempting to remove a bait from the hook. I was to be called for lunch at 1 o'clock and the Hall clock signalled that hour without a carp having obliged with a run, so I threw in a few gentles and cast a new bait, leaving three small coils of line on the water to ensure free running and cocked an ear for the lunch gong. After some minutes watching I noticed that one of the coils had disappeared, the second did likewise to be followed by the third. My shaking hand applied the 'pull' with gratifying results.

Five minutes later my niece, who had been sent to warn me that lunch was getting cold, witnessed my struggles to net a carp weighing a little over three pounds. (I say struggles, for I have only one arm.) It was by now a quarter to two and zero hour for home was two o'clock. Should I cancel arrangements? No! I went back to the house and finished packing. I might have had a record catch that day. Who knows? Anyway, I had my Christmas Carp.

I am indebted to Mr Giles Owen, F.R.Met.Soc., for the meteorological information relating to the locality at the times in question and though there was a sharp rise in temperature to about 45^0F in the minimum grass temperature corresponding to the November capture there seems to be no evidence to explain the Christmas incident unless the carp had some instinctive fore-knowledge of the prolonged cold spell which was to follow.

Christmas Carp - Again
'Faddist'

In Mr J. K. Ebblewhite's interesting and informative article 'Christmas Carp' he records an experience which 'shook him', the capture of a 'Christmas' carp; and describes also a successful day's carp fishing in November. Anglers who keep an eye on winter carp fishing possibilities will be grateful to Mr Ebblewhite for his information; others will read with interest and surprise and maybe count the captures flukes. The idea that the winter carp angler is a 'come inside' guy, dies hard!

I have done more than a little spade work in stressing the winter possibilities of carp fishing. Carp are held to pass the winter in a state of hibernation, or semi-hibernation, and, on this account, are seldom fished for during the cold months. But, every winter, more especially during warmish spells of weather, and after floods, carp break their fast - their hibernation, if you will - and are caught by anglers, admittedly sometimes more by accident than design. Anglers keen enough to try out this winter carping, carefully selecting time and place, may be rewarded handsomely. Almost certainly the favourable factors are relatively high water temperature following warmish spells of weather, and major disturbances caused by floods. Proof? Certainly.

Mr A. B. Arnold recorded the following carp caught in December, 1934: Dec. 10, fifteen; Dec. 11, fifteen; Dec. 12, fourteen; Dec. 17, seventeen; Dec. 18, twelve; total 73. All sizeable fish, some scaling well over 4lb. Bread paste, the bait. Tackle: light fly rod, fine undressed silk line, cast of fine gut substitute, ledger bullet (size of a pea), No. 7 crystal hook to fine gut and small porcupine quill float.

To show that the catches instanced are not mere flukes, I give some extracts from the lists of heavy winter (November - mid-March) carp. These fish weighing 10lb and over, were captured in recent seasons; a point of interest being that some of them were taken from still waters. This is contrary to the view expressed in certain quarters that winter carp are to be had only from rivers and that in still waters the period of hibernation is unbroken.

Some Fine Winter Carp

Captured	Captor	Weight		From
		lb	oz	
Nov. 1933	Mr W. Webster	10	13	Private Water
Nov. 1933	Mr W. Webster	14	8	Private Water
Jan. 1934	Mr R. H. Hill	13	9	Cowbridge
Jan. 1934	Mr J. Leedel	13	8	Cowbridge
Jan. 1934	Mr E. Speight	13	8	Aqueduct (Boston)
Jan. 1934	Mr J. Leedel	12	8	Cowbridge
Jan. 1934	Mr H. Gothard	12	0	Aqueduct (Boston)
Feb. 1935	Mr J. Hayward	11	8	Langport, Somerset
Nov. 1935	Mr S. W. Fox	10	1	Horsham, Sussex
Nov. 1935	Mr H. W. Smith	10	0	Crystal Palace Lake
Nov. 1938	Mr P. Heather	14	8	Crystal Palace Lake
Mar. 1939	Mr W. Carter	14	6	Thames, Cookham
Feb. 1940	Mr G. T. Robinson	18	8	Pit, Huntsmoor Park, Cowley, Middlesex
Nov. 1946	Mr S. F. F. Brown	17	0	Thorpe (gravel pit)
Feb 1947	Mr S. Cerrel	12	2	Lancaster Canal

Mr Richard's Record Carp

Angling, January 1952

Records have been toppling like skittles during the past few months, if all claims made are to be accepted. Regarding one of these, however, there is no room for doubt.

Since Albert Buckley caught his then record 26lb carp at Mapperley reservoir in 1930, other fish weighing close on this weight have been reported from the famous Dagenham lake in Essex; and it has been confidently expected that a new record would be set up by a fish from this water.

The vagaries of angling fortune have, however, annulled this expectation, and the new record carp was taken from an obscure water at Bernithan Court, Llangarren, near Ross-on-Wye, by R. D. Richards, of Gloucester, on October 3rd, 1951. Writing to us regarding this magnificent specimen, Mr Richards gives the following particulars:

The fish, which tipped the beam at 31lb 4oz, was weighed on Avery platform scales with a graduated balance arm, at Bernithan Court, and witnessed by the owner Mrs Barnardiston.

This weight was checked subsequently in Gloucester by Mr John Thorpe, who also verified the dimensions of the carp as 31 inches long (measured from the tip of the snout to the fork of the tail) and its greatest girth as 27 inches.

A scale from the fish was subsequently read by Mr P. C. Austin of Birmingham, who reports:

The fish was 14 years old, it first spawned at 5 years and irregularly afterwards. The last three years showed slow growth. There is practically no erosion which indicates clean water and a healthy fish.

The age quoted by Mr Austin is interesting in view of the fact that Lt-Col Barnardiston placed the first fifty small carp in the lake on March 10th, 1934. Any fish surviving from this original stock would therefore be over seventeen years old. From this it would appear that Mr Richards' fish was one of their progeny. This leaves room for the belief that some of the original fish may still be in the water, and it is reasonable to suppose that they will be even heavier specimens. Will the record be broken again by another fish from this three-acre pool, we wonder?

In this connection Mr Richards states that during the time he was fishing (11am to 4.45pm) he hooked six fish, caught three and lost three, two of which broke his tackle and one 'came unstuck'. And he comments: 'The 31lb 4oz fish was the last of a very exciting day.'

Could the two which broke him have been heavier fish from the original stock? Time alone may answer that question. There is another very interesting aspect of this capture, namely, despite the fact that Mr Richards was using a roach rod, 6.1lb breaking strain line and a No. 10 eyed hook tied direct to the line, which was loaded with a bored bullet about 2 feet from the hook; he brought this monster to gaff in fifteen minutes. Our recollection is that Mr Buckley's 26lb Mapperley fish kept him busy for the best part of an hour. Mr Richards must therefore have been either extremely lucky or super skilful, or was it both?

It is, we think, unfortunate that the fish was gaffed. Mr Richards says: 'The fish was gaffed at 3.45pm and weighed at about 5.30.' That may have meant an appreciable loss of weight.

And what was on the hook, you ask .. ? 'Plain bread paste dipped in English honey,' is the answer. And who witnessed the actual capture? 'Eric Higgs, son of one of the estate staff.' The fish is of course being set up.

There then is the story of a capture which may well retain its record status for many a year to come.

'Carp Fever'

Harry Brotherton

Although my name is not a household word in the angling world, I am a reasonably successful fisherman. I have caught roach, rudd dace and chub which have been chalked up on the specimen board at the club. And I have caught pike and perch which were at least large enough to justify the use of a frying pan. I remember also an occasion when, by the exercise of skill and the self-sacrifice of a pike, I won a contest. There have, moreover, been occasions when I have caught trout. But as this was accomplished with the aid of a worm, which I understand is on a par with the rankest poaching, the less I say about it the better.

There are three fish, however, that I have not caught as yet: the salmon, because the circumference of my bank-roll is too small; the barbel, because within measurable distance of my home there are no barbel to catch; and the carp because – well – your guess is as good as mine. By carp, I mean of course a specimen worthy of the name *Cyprinus Carpio*, not one of those diminutive objects.

My lack of success with carp has caused me to have an annual attack of 'carp fever' which usually begins early in June. Then it is I announce to my brother that 'I intend to catch a carp *this* season!' First I wade through the carp chapters of every angling book on my shelf. This is purely habit as I can recite most of the contents of these volumes. Then when the season approaches I mix large quantities of ground-bait as prescribed, and in the week preceding the opening day I make a regular pilgrimage to a weed-grown water not far from my home. I know that there *are* substantial carp in this water, because a friend catches them with monotonous regularity, one a year, to be exact. I select a swim and while the swans are engaged elsewhere I dump in my offering, repeating the dose at a regular time once in each twenty-four hours. Thus the stage is set.

Then comes the opening day and I am up at an hour which would give a cock something to crow about, and hurry to the pool, in case some casual roach fisher should unwittingly annex my baited swim. I tackle up a hundred yards from the bank and approach as if I were arriving home very late from a club outing. At water's edge I fix up my treble and par-boiled potato according to Cocker, and swing the bait gently into the swim as the distant church clock strikes five. Then there I sit like a statue, but nothing happens.

After a couple of hours of this, I begin to feel that I could cast a trout-fly upon the waters of the Irwell at Manchester with a greater degree of expectation. I decide to try a knob of sweetened paste, from which it is but a short step via the worm to the humble maggot, and before I know where I am; I'm roach fishing and the season is in full swing. I have rid myself of 'carp fever' for another year.

Last year, however, I had great hopes at the worm stage. Just as the end of my patience hove in sight, the loop of line which I had laid out on the bank began to disappear with startling rapidity. I counted ten in about half a second, then tightened on my fish. It felt as though I had hooked a wringing machine, and in my mind's eye, I could see the expression on my friend's face when I dumped a big carp on the club bar that evening. But that fish decided to make a dash through the overhanging branches of a willow, and there wasn't a thing I could do about it. The vision of my triumphant entry into the club was fading when the fish turned and came back by the same route. Mentally I mounted the club steps again. After what seemed an age (three minutes to be exact), the brute surfaced and for the first time I saw my carp, but it was a pike!

This was not the end, for about an hour later a youngster who was fishing nearby called for my assistance. In spite of his crude tackle he had hooked and was weeded by a good fish. It was a carp of some five pounds weight. And the boy explained that he was fishing for pike baits. I ask you!

Yes, I think I'll give it up as a bad job, this big carp catching. It seems to me that to hook one is nothing short of a miracle; and having seen an angler hook and lose a big one in a Shropshire pool I've come to the conclusion that another miracle is necessary if one is to land a hooked carp. To expect twin miracles to happen on the same day is asking too much.

If by some remote chance I scoop the football pools I may catch a salmon. If by an even more remote chance I ever persuade my wife to forsake her beloved Blackpool to go on a fishing holiday in the South, I may catch a barbel, but to catch a really big carp is, I'm beginning to think, too remote a chance ever to be a possibility.

But wait, I wonder how I should fare if I baited my treble with a 'King Edward' instead of the usual 'Cheshire Early'. I'll try it next year!

Sources

The Carpe, *Leonard Mascall.* From *A Booke of Fishing with Hooke & Line, and of all other instruments thereunto belonging,* John Wolfe, 1590.

A Welsh Carp Lake, *H. T. Sheringham.* From *An Open Creel,* 1910.

Carp and their Curious Habits, *Frans Domhof.* From the *Fishing Gazette,* October, 1954.

Alfred Mackrill's Grand Carp. *Anon*

Overbeck's Monster, *Horace Hutchinson.* From *Country Life, 1904.*

Among the Carp, *G. Christopher Davies.* From *Angling Idylls,* Chapman & Hall, 1876.

A Carp in the Night, *Gerry Berth-Jones.* From *The Angling Times Book,* James Barrie, 1955.

The Susceptible Carp, *J.H. Keene.* From *The Practical Fisherman,* 1881.

A Taste of the Dairymaid, *G. Brennand.* From *Walton's Delight,* 1953.

The Appeal of the Carp, *Michael Shephard.* From *Come and Fish, 1952.*

Queer Fishing, *H. T. Sheringham.* From *A Book of Fishing Stories,* Aflalo, 1913.

Carp, *'Otter'.* From *The Modern Angler,* Upcott Gill, 1898.

Fishes of the Carp Kind, *'Piscator' (William Hughes).* From *The Practical Angler,* Simpkin, Marshall & Co., 1842.

Carp from a Puddle near the Sea, *Dave Marlborough.* From *Angling,* June 1964.

When The Carp Fed Like Roach, *Peter Tombleson.* From *Angling,* 1963.

The Fish With A Sixth Sense, *Dick Kefford.* From *Angling,* 1963.

Carp In South Africa, *J.H. Yates.* From *Angling,* September 1953.

A Carp From Mapperley Shallows, *John Norman.* From *Angling,* August 1953.

Christmas Carp, *J.K. Ebblewhite.* From *Angling,* November/Dec 1947.

Christmas Carp - Again, *'Faddist'.* From *Angling,* March/April 1948.

Mr Richard's Record Carp. From *Angling,* January 1952.

Carp Fever, *Harry Brotherton.* From *Angling,* September 1951.